MARKETING
WORKS

Unlocking

Big Company

Strategies

for Small

Business

CHRIS LEE & DANIELE LIMA

DEDICATIONS

For Chris Lee:

To my lovely wife Elaine and my son Eugene.

For Daniele Lima:

To my wonderful parents Lidia and Giuseppe,
to whom I owe everything. Thank you.

MARKETING
WORKS

Unlocking

Big Company

Strategies

for Small

Business

MARKETING WORKS

ISBN: 1-60037-009-8   (Paperback)

Published by:
MORGAN · JAMES
THE ENTREPRENEURIAL PUBLISHER ™

Morgan James Publishing, LLC
1225 Franklin Ave Ste 325
Garden City, NY 11530-1693
Toll Free 800-485-4943
www.MorganJamesPublishing.com

Cover and Interior Design by:
Tony Laidig
www.thecoverexpert.com
tony@thecoverexpert.com

All charactertures within the book are by Ching Ling Lee.
All enquiries to: chinglinglee@hotmail.com

PREFACE

With the business environment becoming increasingly competitive, it is clear that to succeed it is critical for your business to have an edge over your numerous and in many cases, larger competitors. This edge, available to all small businesses, is marketing.

The aims of this book are to examine the key aspects of marketing with the emphasis squarely on small business, and to demonstrate how a marketing approach can be used to improve the performance and subsequent profitability of your business.

The word "business" may denote risk. No one can ensure the success of any business venture. Effective marketing, however, when properly implemented, can maximise the strengths of your business and help you capitalise on the available opportunities, while minimising the level of risk.

What makes this book unique then? Simply that the tried and tested marketing principles used by successful marketing managers are explained in a way that can be easily adapted for your individual business needs.

ACKNOWLEDGEMENTS

This book represents a ten-year journey of discovery and challenges, traveled more easily, with the help of mentors, the list of which has grown too long to mention.

It is important, however, to thank a number of key people from different organisations who have graciously allowed us to use their words, insight and experience.

Specific thanks go to the following people for their respective input into the book:

Mark Smith	Managing Director - Cadbury Schweppes, Australia & New Zealand
Kevin Panozza	Managing Director - Sales Force, Australia
Michael Morrison	Research Director of the Australian Centre for Retail Studies
Martin Lindstrom	Managing Director – Lindstrom Company, Denmark & Australia
John Mazzotta	Accredited Family Law specialist Lander & Rogers, Australia
Richard Webb	President of Nielsen /

	Net Ratings in Asia Pacific / Latin America.
Dr. Elisabet Wreme	Group Manager – Sensis Search, Australia
Leo Kerema	Corporate Brand Manager – Bluescope Steel Ltd., Australia.

Constructive criticism and open feedback from others have also helped substantially in focusing the content in this book.

Finally our ongoing and sincere thanks go out to everyone who has helped us realise a dream of articulating our passion for marketing in this book. Our hope is that it can serve to help many small businesses grow to their full potential.

TABLE OF CONTENTS

CHAPTER 1

WHY YOU NEED MARKETING

There are many small businesses everywhere that consistently outperform the markets they operate in, as well as enjoy strong, ongoing profitability. There are also countless other small businesses that consistently fail to do either of these things and routinely add to the frighteningly high mortality rate of small businesses.

Yet in spite of this, many small business owners faced with declining sales and profitability continue to resist changes to their traditional approach to business management. Perhaps the key reason for this resistance to change is simply fear of the unknown.

In this chapter the most commonly asked questions and objections regarding marketing will be looked at, with the aim of clarifying any misconceptions about the value of marketing for you and your business.

KEEP IN MIND

The most difficult step in adopting a marketing approach for your business is simply to have the courage to begin.

FREQUENTLY ASKED QUESTIONS

1. Marketing: What does it really mean?

First, it is not the same as selling. Selling is when you have a product you want to provide to the market, whereas marketing is when you have a product that the market wants. In other words, marketing is about voluntary exchange. It caters specifically to an **unmet customer need**, and done in a way that is appropriate for your customer group.

Therefore, you must know exactly what your customers want. By knowing your customers' needs and supplying a product that meets those needs, you are in a far better position to sell your product

2. Marketing: Is it available to all small businesses and if so, at what cost?

The answer to the first part of the question is most definitely, yes. The fact is that the benefits from marketing activities and research methods are available and applicable to all small businesses.

The cost of **marketing information** will vary depending on the nature and magnitude of the data required. It is fair to say, however, that few small businesses could justify spending vast amounts on marketing activities, which the large national and multi-national corporations are compelled to spend in order to remain competitive with their main rivals.

Thankfully, the marketing information needs of a small business are considerably smaller and can usually be obtained inexpensively (or in some cases for free), with minimal effort.

The main sources of marketing information that are available will be discussed later in the book.

3. Marketing: I've always done well without it, so do I really need it now?

Again the answer to this question is almost certainly, yes. Many businesses do quite well initially, but the statistical reality is that the majority of businesses fail in the first five years.

Some businesses may even achieve acceptable levels of profit. In many cases, however, this level of profitability could be significantly improved with the adoption of a marketing approach. Similarly, other businesses may have succeeded due to little or no competition initially. But with imminent new rivals waiting in the wings, no business can remain complacent for too long.

A business that embraces a marketing approach can develop an increased capacity to:

- Define existing market knowledge and identify information gaps.

- Plan and allocate resources, leaving no resource idle.

- Gain as much control as possible over future market developments.

4. If I adopt a marketing approach, will I lose any advantages my business currently holds?

The answer is a resounding "no!!" The reluctance to fix something 'when it ain't broke' is understandable, but this fear is unfounded with respect to the marketing approach discussed in this book.

The marketing activities in this book have been carefully thought out and designed. If implemented appropriately, they will align with and complement your current positive business practices, ensuring that all of your business resources are fully utilised for maximum impact.

At best, your current business strengths will be enhanced and at worst maintained, but would never diminish below current levels of profitability, when you adopt an appropriate marketing strategy.

5. How long does it take to implement a marketing approach?

Once you decide to implement a marketing approach for your business the actual process of marketing is fairly straightforward. For most existing businesses, the development and integration of an appropriate marketing plan will happen gradually. There is no specific timeframe that must be adhered to. Generally, however, it is in the interest of the business to move as quickly as possible, but ultimately, whether you decide to take two weeks or two years, it is up to you.

This book will outline a step-by-step marketing process that you can adopt at your own pace.

KEEP IN MIND

No business has a right to success. It must continually earn the right to survive by continuing to effectively meet consumer needs.

SUMMARY

- When a business fails, it is highly likely that the needs of the customer have been forgotten or misconstrued.

- Resisting appropriate change can become an expensive exercise.

- A sophisticated and informed consumer has evolved. They know what they want. Any business that is unwilling or unable to respond quickly and effectively to these customers is likely to fail in the longer term.

CHAPTER 2

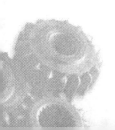

MARKETING PLANNING PROCESS

This chapter will introduce the **Marketing Planning Process**, which can be customized for your business. By using this simple model your business will have a stronger marketing focus and gain from all the benefits inherent in a marketing approach.

The marketing planning process is divided into four stages (see figure 2.1) where each stage answers one key question:

Stage A: **Comprehensive Analysis:** What position is your business in now?

Stage B: **Objectives Module:** Where would you like the business to be?

Stage C: **Marketing Blueprint:** How do you get to this new position?

Stage D: **Feedback Module:** Has your business got to where it should be?

10 Great Marketing Tips For Your Business

- Know exactly what your customers want.

- Listen to your customers before you do the talking.

- Respect your customers.

- Look for groups of customers with similar unmet needs.

- Be honest about the strengths and weaknesses of your business.

- Strengthen areas of relative weakness.

- Observe the market to capture early opportunities.

- Always exhaust available data before paying for research.

- Reward those people who contribute to your success.

- Enjoy the journey and learn from the ups and the downs.

STAGE A:
COMPREHENSIVE ANALYSIS:
"What position is your business in now?"

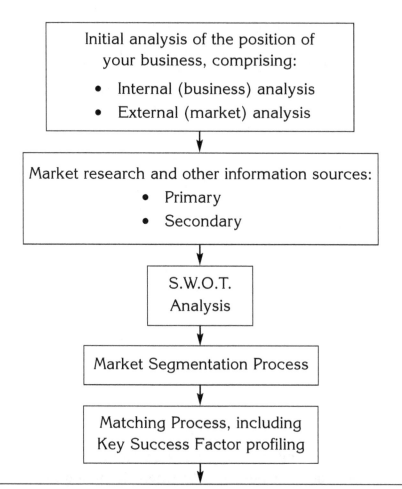

Initial analysis of the position of
your business, comprising:

- Internal (business) analysis
- External (market) analysis

Market research and other information sources:
- Primary
- Secondary

S.W.O.T.
Analysis

Market Segmentation Process

Matching Process, including
Key Success Factor profiling

- Select specific market segments to be targeted
- Identify exactly the unmet customer needs

Proceed to Stage B

Figure 2.1: Marketing Planning Process

STAGE B:
OBJECTIVES MODULE:
"Where would you like the business to be?"

- Set your business objectives
- Estimate possible risks and potential upsides for these objectives
- List the key assumptions you made when developing the above objectives

STAGE C:
MARKETING BLUEPRINT:
"How do you get to this new position?"

Develop a specific marketing blueprint. Include:

- all strategies for the product itself, its distribution, pricing and promotion

- all resource allocation details

- time related details

- cost estimates

STAGE D:
FEEDBACK FUNCTION:
"Has your business got to where it should be?"

- Ongoing evaluation of actual performance against planned performance to highlight any variances

- Analysis of variances to enhance future planning and performance

Figure 2.1: Marketing Planning Process (continued)

CHAPTER 3

STAGE A:
COMPREHENSIVE ANALYSIS

Stage A of the marketing planning process, also known as the comprehensive analysis, answers the question: "What position is your business in now?" and comprises a number of steps (see Figure 2.1). Stage A is critical to the business because it forms the basis for the **marketing blueprint**, which will be discussed in Chapter 5.

Within Stage A is the Initial Analysis which evaluates both the business and the market within which the business operates. This analysis is based on the marketing information which is already available or which can be easily obtained. Ultimately, this analysis will help you to identify the strengths and weaknesses of your business, as well as the opportunities and threats that exist in that market. From this analysis, any viable market segments in the market can be identified.

A **matching process** is then used to match the capabilities of the business with customer needs. This serves two purposes. First, this will identify the most viable of the market segments. Secondly, the key factors to achieve success in these segments will be uncovered.

3.1   THE INITIAL ANALYSIS

The objective of the Initial Analysis is to identify and evaluate the main characteristics and trends in the market that your business operates in with a view to more fully understanding what your business needs to do to be successful in that market. As well, the analysis looks internally at your business to understand what it needs to do to best align its operations with the current dynamics of the market.

This analysis is based on information obtained through various sources including those from the business itself e.g. sales data, customer analysis and cost structures. It is also based on information of the industry as a whole, including data on overall market size, changes in market needs over time, competition and technological advancements. The sources for both types of information will be discussed later in this chapter.

If performed well, the Initial Analysis can reveal a lot about what is happening both in the market and in your business, and most importantly shed some light as to why. Therefore, you will be able to gain valuable insights and respond quickly and effectively to any changes, as they are occurring. If performed badly, the inaccurate information will inevitably lead to ineffective marketing strategies. That is why it is important that all data used in the analysis is up-to-date and relevant.

KEEP IN MIND

An arrow no matter how straight it flies can never hit its mark if it is originally shot off target.

3.1.1 WHAT BUSINESS ARE YOU REALLY IN?

The first thing that the initial analysis sets out to do is to answer the question, "What business are you really in?"

On face of it, this may appear to be an absurd question to ask. Certainly, you can tell what market your business operates in. For example, the book market, the shoe market, the menswear market, and so on. However, this is not enough. You must also know exactly what **market segment** your business caters to. For instance, based on the examples given above, your business might be in:

1. The educational book market for primary and secondary level schools, but not tertiary (as part of the overall book market).

2. The high-end fashion, leather shoe market catering only for women and not men (as part of the overall shoe market).

3. Affordable, medium quality/medium priced menswear clothing and accessories (as part of the overall menswear market).

In each of these three examples, the business operates in one segment and not in all segments of their respective markets. Constructing a profile with key descriptors about your business will help you to identify the specific segment to which your business belongs. You may want to create this profile by using a checklist of 'who, what, when, why and how' regarding your customers and their needs.

Checklist of key questions:

- Who are your main customers currently?

- What other potential customers could be targeted by your business?

- What are the main products (goods or services) sold by your business to the current customers?
- What key needs are met by these products?
- What other products could your business supply to its customers?
- When do your customers mainly buy?
- Why do they buy the products to begin with?
- How do they buy (buying patterns and methods)?
- Why do they buy from your business?
- What don't your customers like about buying from your business?
- What related items do they buy elsewhere and why?

EXAMPLE

The owner of a small, but profitable computer programming company considered that his business catered to no particular market segment. He believed that his customers were evenly distributed across all industries. On closer examination, however, the owner discovered to his surprise that about 40% of his customers were accounting firms. This realization prompted the company to target this area more rigorously, with the result being an increased clientele list and increased profitability.

What happened here? Over time, the business had developed a superior and specialized knowledge of accounting systems in direct response to customer needs. Because the specialization was gradual, this market segment was not identified until an analysis of the business was conducted.

3.1.2 THINK BROADLY ABOUT THE BUSINESS YOU ARE IN

Once you have determined exactly what business you are really in, the next step is to take a broader look at what (beyond the actual product) the customers are buying from you.

Have a look at the three columns in this example. In the first column, the names of a number of well-known businesses are listed. The second column displays their respective product offerings. It is, however, more important to identify what the customer is actually buying beyond the product itself. This is found in the third column.

Business	Product Offering	What's in It for the Customer?
Universal	Movies	Entertainment
Revlon Cosmetics	Make-up	Beauty
Telstra	Telephones	Communication
Carrier	Air-conditioning	Comfort
Mt Buller	Skiing	Recreation
Metrail	Trains/Trams/Buses	Convenience
Coca-Cola	Soft drink	Acceptance
Club Med	Travel & Tourism	Escape

From this type of analysis, the broader offering of a business is quickly revealed.

Consider the Cadbury Schweppes Company. Their product offerings are confectionery, food and beverages. But what are the customers really buying?

Mark Smith (Managing Director of Cadbury Schweppes—Australia & New Zealand), said: "I work for an outstanding company. And I'm really passionate about what we do, which put simply, is to bring delight into the lives of millions of consumers."

Therefore, Cadbury Schweppes is in the business of putting joy and fun into people's lives. Not just to sell confectionery, food and beverages.

The customer's perception of your product can be more important than the product itself. Coca-Cola is a classic example of this. The long-term popularity of the Coca-Cola drink has been sustained over many decades. This would suggest that there is more to the drink than its taste. The advertising is perennially the same and is targeted at young people. "Coke is it" really says, "Drink it and with it comes acceptance, status and fun." Not bad for a soft drink.

Similarly, once it was established by Revlon that women are really buying 'beauty,' Revlon tailored the marketing strategies, packaging and advertising to rein-force this perception.

By understanding what a customer really wants to buy, your marketing strategies and promotions will more accu-rately hit the mark.

KEEP IN MIND

- In reality, you do not sell a product, but rather the perception of satisfaction and positive experience. The customer buys the perfectly drilled hole in the wall, not the drill.

- Good experiences mean repeat buying and bad experiences mean lost customers and earnings both now and in the future.

3.1.3 INTERNAL BUSINESS ANALYSIS

The **Internal Business Analysis** examines the business and its internal workings. It aims to evaluate the respective strengths and weaknesses of the business. Unlike the **External Market Analysis** that evaluates external opportunities and threats that your business has no direct control over, internal strengths and weaknesses are what you can control and, therefore, directly influence.

As the business manager you need to ask yourself questions that will aid you with this analysis.

Checklist of key questions:

By Customer:

1. Who do you actively define as your target market?

By Product:

2. What products do you offer your target market to meet their needs?

3. How many of each product do you sell?

4. When do you sell your products (i.e. time of year, month, week, day etc)?

5. What are the strengths of each product line?

6. Which products don't sell well? Why?

7. What alternative products could you sell to take the place of those that do not sell well?

8. At what price do you sell your products?

9. What is the gross margin for each product?

10. How much does each product net after all costs (including promotional costs)?

11. What other products could the business sell to supplement its existing range?

12. What products could be deleted from the current product range? Why?

By Resource:

13. What key resources from your business drive its sales and growth?

14. Who are the key business personnel? What are the key skills they bring to the business?

15. Do you have a succession plan for the promotion or loss of any key personnel?

16. What additional training do current employees need for both current and future roles?

17. What additional staff and/or skills do you need to bring into the business?

18. Is your equipment (i.e. machinery, plant, etc) adequate for current and projected needs?

19. What additional level of borrowings are you able to access if required?

By Comparison with Key Rivals:

20. How does the quality of your product range (including all goods and services), compare to your main rivals?

21. What unique skills or knowledge does your business have, that your rivals do not have?

22. What general advantages does your business have compared to the competition?

23. Are these advantages effectively turned to profit? How? If not, why?

This list of suggested questions is by no means exhaustive. These questions are designed to raise many more to allow a complete evaluation of all aspects of your business. From this analysis you will be able to determine the strengths and weaknesses of your business, which will form part of the **S.W.O.T Analysis**, to be discussed later in this chapter.

3.1.4 CUSTOMER ANALYSIS & RETENTION - THE KEY TO ONGOING SUCCESS.

One of the most important tasks for a business is to accurately assess who the customers are and the extent of their loyalty. Customers can be classified within the Customer Analysis Model (Figure 3.1).

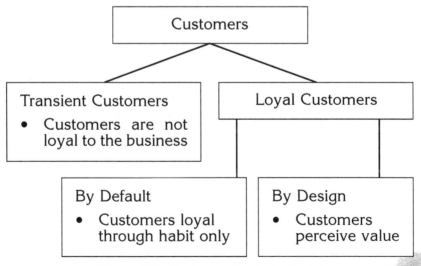

Figure 3.1: Customer Analysis Model

Where do most of your customers currently fit?

From the model, you can see there are three categories of customers:

- Transient customers who are clearly not loyal to the business.

- Customers who are loyal by default (usually out of habit).

- Customers who are loyal by design because their needs are being met and, therefore, place real value in dealing with your business.

It is important to determine where your various customers fit because your actions for each group will vary. Let us now examine the key aspects of each of the three groups.

Customer Type	Rationale for Customer Behavior	What Else do You Need to Know?	Implications and Next Action Steps for the Business
Customers who are loyal to the business by design.	These customers are clear on the value they receive from the business.

These customers are often brand focused. | Specifically which particular services or products are providing that value to the customer?

What else can be offered to further meet the needs of these customers? | The 80-20 rule (also known as Pareto's Law) means this group drives your profitability.

Do all you can to retain this group of customers.

Recognize the loyalty of this group and reward them to strengthen the bond further. |

Customers who are loyal to the business through habit.	These customers are only loyal because it is more effort to change. This means that when a contract finishes or a competitor changes their mix to offer a more attractive option, the customer may leave. The rationale may be price-related too, but is often not.	Find out what the unmet needs are.	Conduct research with this group to find out what the business needs to change and why. Reward them for this information and insight. Give assurances that the situation will be improved to better meet their needs.
Transient customers, who are neither loyal nor consistent.	These customers do business with you irregularly. For any number of possible reasons they go elsewhere some or a lot of the time. In some cases they never return. This may be a geographical issue or some other seasonal or cyclical variation, which means it is more comfortable for the customer to buy from you sometimes and not others.	What factors are causing customers either to not return at all or return only infrequently? Are these causes related to the staff, or any other aspect of the business? This includes pricing, range of products and services, shopping hours, terms of credit, parking facilities, after sales service, etc.	Once reasons for the transience are determined, examine ways of addressing these issues positively. Determine the cost versus benefit of making any changes. Decide if the changes are worth implementing, and promote any proposed changes to the market.

* Note: The 80-20 rule (i.e. Pareto's Law) means that a small number (20%) of key customers are responsible for a large proportion (80%) of the business profits. Therefore, it is important to recognize the loyalty of this customer group and reward them.

EXAMPLE

Accredited Family Law Specialist, John Mazzotta from a leading law firm, Lander & Rogers recognized the loyalty of a number of his clients. These key clients refer a significant amount of work to John. He sought to reward them in a way that reflected their importance to his business.

This signal of gratitude took a number of forms ranging from rebates, gift vouchers, offers of free educational seminars in relevant legal areas and opportunities to attend sought after cultural and sporting events.

This is a simple example of recognizing and rewarding key customers who contribute to business performance.

Each business needs to conduct its own customer analysis and implement a program to reward the key accounts in a way that is both practical and ethical.

Although larger companies have been keen to reward new customers in order to expand their customer base, they are now beginning to realize the value of the longer-term customer.

Loyal customers are worth around five times more than new customers. In an article from "Professional Marketing" (February 2005), Amanda Swinburn reported that large businesses have quantified the actual dollars that loyal customers bring in. For example, Ford has calculated that a loyal customer is worth $142,000 over the life time of that customer and Domino's Pizza have reported a loyal customer over 10 years will generate $5,000.

Perform the simple exercise below to help channel your thoughts on how and when you can best reward key customer groups for their ongoing support.

Names of key contributing customers or customer groups	What do these Icustomers bring to the business?	How can these customers be rewarded?	What might be the drawbacks of the rewards program?

3.1.5 EXTERNAL MARKET ANALYSIS

The external market analysis involves a thorough analysis of the market, where the current trends and characteristics are identified and analyzed. This is to ensure that internal marketing strategies are not developed and implemented in isolation from external market forces.

Given a specific set of market conditions, a marketing blueprint might work well today. The same blueprint, however, a year later may be a complete disaster because the environment may have changed significantly.

These variable factors when analyzed help determine the main threats and opportunities the business faces. Although the business may have no control over external factors, understanding them will help you put together a more effective marketing blueprint (Stage C, Chapter 5).

These external factors include the competitive climate, cultural and social climate, market size and trends, technological environment, economic climate and legal environment.

Competitive Climate

The competitive climate of a market refers to the number, size, type and behavioral patterns of your rivals. The competitive climate provides insights into the behavior of your competitors.

Some key questions to ask include:

- How many competitors do you directly compete against?

- Who are your main competitors?

- Do your key rivals actively trade with or market to anyone in particular? Why?

- What product range do they have in comparison to you?

- What pricing policies do they adopt? Why? Are they similar or different to yours?

- What (if any) competitive advantage do you have over your rivals?

- What competitive disadvantages do you have compared to your rivals?

- What advertising do they use and why?

- How does your location compare with theirs?

Cultural and Social Climate

The cultural and social climate is very important because it directly affects the way in which people think and feel about various issues. It has a very real and significant impact on buying behavior.

As a successful marketer of a small business, you will need to identify and understand the current customer attitudes and beliefs regarding issues of ethics, values, religion, cultural diversity etc. and how they may impact your business.

Consider the following examples:

Traditionally, certain foods have been regarded as tasteless and boring and, therefore, relatively unpopular. A prime example of this is the range of all-bran products.

Recently, it was found that the soluble fiber in all-bran products reduces the level of cholesterol in the body. This previously unfashionable product range has since found acceptability among health conscious customers, in light of the high level of publicity about the dangers of high cholesterol levels. Statistical analysis shows that demand for such products has risen significantly.

Restaurants, health food stores and sandwich bars are just some of the small businesses affected by this change in attitude and subsequent change in consumer demand. Clearly, by understanding consumer attitudes and beliefs, derived from the social and cultural climate, your business will be better able to anticipate and respond to emerging trends in the market place.

Market Size and Trends

Another uncontrollable factor is market size and the overall market trends. In other words, how large is the market pertinent to your business and is it a shrinking or growing market? These observations can be made from the perspective of the entire market in question and/or from the point of view of the particular segment your business operates in.

It is possible to have a situation where the overall market is large and growing in size, but certain segments within that market may be shrinking.

An example of this is the computer market. Overall it is an enormously large market and expanding rapidly, however the medium size computers are now being replaced with smaller, more powerful personal computers and laptops.

Another example is that of the television market. In absolute terms, this market is growing and yet the segment of non-digital televisions is shrinking in market value, as consumers gain a greater understanding of the benefits of digital televisions.

As well as current market size and trend analysis, another piece of information, which is both useful and available in some markets, is an industry projection, which attempts to forecast what will happen in the market over the next twelve months. Industry projection will be discussed later in this chapter under "Sources of Marketing Information."

Technological Environment

The technology employed in each industry is important because the more appropriately advanced it is, the more productive the other business resources will become. A skilled dressmaker can produce a greater number of dresses per day using modern fabric cutting and sewing machines, than by using slower and less precise machines.

The dress designers would also be able to design many more dress patterns in a given time using a CAD system (i.e. a computer assisted design system), rather than adopting the more conventional method of pen to paper.

Remember that even if you decide to take advantage of any new relevant technology, there is no guarantee your competitors will not update their business technology as well, if they have not already done so.

In real terms by improving your business technologically, you will achieve parity with key rivals, not necessarily superiority. However, if you do not routinely update your technological base to match the market, you will most assuredly put your business back.

Economic Climate

The economic climate has a huge influence on the running of any business, regardless of how well positioned your product is.

If, for example, the economy is going through an economic downturn, the customer's willingness and ability to buy will decrease. Therefore, demand for certain products may decrease substantially. Typically, products perceived to be luxury items will suffer most in these circumstances. Conversely, when economic conditions are favorable, people generally have a higher level of **discretionary income** and willingness to spend.

By its very nature, the economy is dynamic and constantly changing. The shrewd marketer must protect the business by keeping a constant vigil over the various, key economic indicators such as **inflation rate, interest rates, currency exchange rate, unemployment rate and economic growth rate**. By being aware of any changes to these key indicators, you will be in a better position to respond quickly with appropriate changes to your marketing strategies.

If your product range is a necessity and/or relatively inexpensive, then economic downturns would likely only have a marginal effect on the business. On the other hand, if the product is perceived to be a luxury item and is fairly expensive, then the business can expect a negative impact on overall demand. Consequently, a strategy to lessen the impact will have to be employed, the most obvious being to lower the price.

On the face of it, a hot bread store would be less likely affected by an economic recession than an up-market giftware store located in the same shopping center. However, the gift shop could minimize the challenges by adjusting its pricing policies and/or promotional incentive offers, thereby differentiating the product range on one or two grounds.

Overall, it is vital to keep your finger on the pulse of the economic climate and respond quickly and effectively to any ups and downs.

The Legal Environment

The small business owner must have a clear understanding of all legal requirements when formulating marketing strategies and plans. Breaching these laws can lead to both civil and in more serious cases, criminal prosecutions.

In Australia with the advent and growth of **consumerism**, the statutes being developed (both at a federal and state level) are formulated to protect the consumer and ensure that their rights are maintained. Increasingly harsh penalties now stand to further discourage dishonest and unfair business practices.

Commissions such as the Trade Practices Commission and the Australian Competition and Consumer Commission (A.C.C.C.) have been established to monitor the business environment and ensure that any reported breaches are investigated and penalized where appropriate, to encourage and maintain an environment of fair, competitive and ethical business practices.

Australian business law also requires businesses to abide by various operating regulations concerning registrations, payment of taxes, licensing arrangements and minimum conditions for employees to mention, but a few. If you're uncertain about any area of business law relating to your business, you would be wise to contact your state or local government office

DANGER

for clarification. Often, it is a fine line between what is deemed to be innovative or creative and unlawful behavior. For example, a business that engages in collective negotiation practices may inadvertently breach price fixing laws.

Current Chairman of the A.C.C.C., Graeme Samuel has publicly encouraged all businesses to be proactive in checking the legality of certain marketing activities, to avoid any inference of anticompetitive behavior. If you have any doubt about the validity of any activity you are involved with, this approach could take your business out of harm's way.

Overall, the legal environment is like any other uncontrollable factor discussed in this section. The successful, small business will recognize these legal rules and regulations and implement appropriate marketing strategies.

TIP FOR LEGAL ADVICE

For free legal information on the web, go to:

www.findlaw.com.au

This leading legal resource has a search engine for your specific issues as well as a specialized business section which covers all aspects of Business Law including: starting and running a business, employment issues, intellectual property and taxation requirements.

The A.C.C.C. also has a useful website:

http://www.accc.gov.au/

SUMMARY

- The Initial Analysis is made up of both the Internal Business Analysis and the External Market Analysis. When properly conducted it gives a good indication of how your business is currently positioned in the prevailing market.

- The Internal Business Analysis will allow you to identify and document the controllable strengths and weaknesses of your business, which can be manipulated to optimally respond to the changing market conditions.

- The External Market Analysis examines the prevailing market characteristics and trends that your business must understand, but has little or no control over.

- To discover what business you are in, go to the essence of your product offering, not necessarily the physical product.

- Decide on what it is that the customer really wants from your product and ensure they are able to receive it.

- You must analyze your key customers and continue to try to move as many as possible into the 'loyal by design' group.

3.2   SOURCES OF MARKET INFORMATION

Information is arguably the most valuable resource available to you in small business. Put simply, sound marketing strategic planning is a direct consequence of good marketing information. Conversely, inadequate or incomplete data will increase the chances of developing a flawed strategy.

This chapter will examine in full the different sources of market information, which are available to your small business. This information can then be used to carry out **market research**.

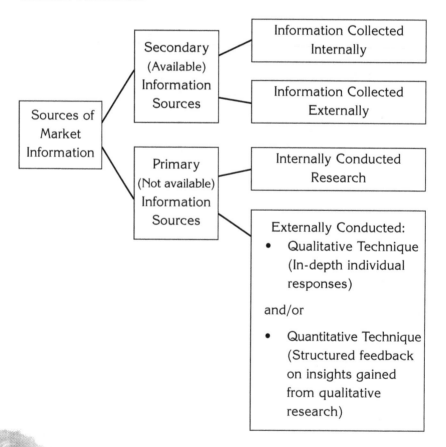

Figure 3.2: Sources of Market Information

3.2.1 SECONDARY INFORMATION

When conducting a **market analysis**, the first type of information you should search out is **Secondary Information**. Secondary Information is information that already exists. In other words, it is information that has already been gathered and is available to your business. This secondary information is divided into two main groups:

- Internally collected secondary information
- Externally collected secondary information

Internally Collected Secondary Information

The internal records of the business activities from both the past and present provide the most fundamental form of market information. Here information is extracted from a number of key sources such as:

- Actual sales figures
- Cost information
- Customer feedback (on any number of issues)
- Supplier conversation records
- Research reports

- Supplier reports

- Staff performance and feedback reports

- Competitor activity reports

Who would have thought listening actually does have its advantages...

From these reports several simple analyses can be routinely performed by the business. For example, detailed sales results over time (both in dollar and unit terms) can provide insight into how individual products, entire product lines, departments, branches, etc. are performing in the market place. These figures can then be viewed over time to illustrate the trends emerging at each level.

Comparative analysis can also be performed where planned versus actual performance can be compared and any variance, whether positive or negative, can be identified.

An analysis can also be performed on the cost information. Again, actual costs can be compared to budgeted costs and variances identified. Cost levels can be viewed over time to highlight significant trends and possible inefficiencies.

Moreover, the effectiveness of marketing activities can be appraised by viewing their impact on sales levels and overall profitability. Did your marketing strategies work? Why or why not? How well did they work? What factors drove the result that was achieved?

In reality, the number and types of analyses that can be performed using internally collected secondary information are endless. You need to choose what is most appropriate for the answers that you want.

Remember that this internal secondary information already exists and is easily found. How you dissect and analyze this information is only limited by your resourcefulness and imagination.

Externally Collected Sources of Secondary Information

Having exhausted all available internal sources of information, the researcher has the subsequent option of using externally collected sources of information.

Externally collected data is very popular and attractive to most small businesses for various reasons. To begin with, the data is easily obtainable by anyone, and detailed and accurate enough to supply the user with relevant and reliable information. Moreover, almost invariably these sources of information are available at little or no cost.

There are countless sources of secondary data available that are directly relevant to small business. Here is a list of a number of typical sources:

- *The Australian Bureau of Statistics*

The Australian Bureau of Statistics is the best source of raw statistical data available to the small business. They have an extensive series of publications on practically any and all economic activity nationally. The statistical information covers many aspects of society such as demographics, economic indicators and social issues.

The first step is to obtain the Australian Bureau of Statistics - Catalogue of Publications, which lists all available material and includes an easy to follow subject index. This publication is available on request from any Australian Bureau of Statistics office.

The most famous research by the Australian Bureau of Statistics is the population census. This tool is invaluable for business planning and decision making. The population census is conducted every five years nationally, and contains statistical data on virtually all variables of the population including age brackets, religion, income distributions, levels of education, marital status, occupational status, levels of discretionary income, and so on.

Detailed statistical data is available not only about the population, but also on all areas of business such as retailing, wholesale and manufacturing.

Website: http://www.abs.gov.au/

EXAMPLE

'Peter' wishing to take advantage of the science fiction craze intends to open up a comic book store and is uncertain of exactly which location would be optimal for this venture. He has several options, but is not certain of the best alternative.

By examining the Australian Bureau of Statistics census information for each of the three areas, he can obtain

EXAMPLE *continued*

information on the number of people in that area and surrounding areas, the age breakdowns, levels of income, discretionary spending levels and so on.

Additionally, he can also obtain information about the number of schools and availability of public transportation in each area, to better define the location for the new business. This same procedure could also be used if he already had an existing business and was doing a feasibility study to see if there was a better location.

EXAMPLE

'Max' operates a small, driving school in a Victorian, rural area. Business had been slow in the first year. He would like to know why.

The key here is not just to ask how many other schools there are, but also, what the age demographics are and whether this region is growing or shrinking in population. In other words, the business needs to find out how many people are about to move into the 16 to 20- age group.

From this analysis, he will be in a much better position to say whether it is wise to continue the business into the future in this area. Or perhaps it would be better to relocate to an area with a more robust population growth rate, especially in the pivotal 16 to 20 age range.

- *Trade Associations*

Trade Associations present a tremendous opportunity to gain timely and relevant data about most aspects of a given industry. For example, a marketer operating a shoe store can examine the information from the relevant trade association and learn which types of shoes are selling, which are not, which particular brands of shoes are doing well, related pricing information, distribution information on channels and retail outlets, etc. This information is usually made available annually and is a prime source of information on what is happening in a particular market or industry.

Australian Trade and Industry Associations Website: http://www.export61.com/

- *Business Indexes*

The most up-to-date information and data relating to a particular business or market can probably be found in periodical articles of the relevant newspapers, trade journals and magazines. These periodicals can be found in business indexes under subject index classification, in alphabetical order.

By looking up a particular subject in the index e.g. small business expenditures, articles relating to this topic will be listed, including the reference for the article.

These business indexes are very useful because the business world is very dynamic with constant change. Books soon become obsolete. Therefore, it is important to monitor contemporary information.

Most academic libraries will hold the major business indexes and the accompanying periodicals. Below is a short list of the four main indexes relevant to Australian small businesses, which are available from major libraries and can be used as a source of up-to-date, externally produced secondary information:

1. Australian Public Affairs Information Service (A.P.A.I.S):

   Australian Public Affairs Information Service is a monthly publication, which indexes its articles alphabetically in subject order. The articles are taken from periodicals and books about business matters and other aspects of Australian society, such as social and cultural changes, legal and political issues and economic affairs. Such a breadth of articles would be helpful in obtaining information for the various uncontrollable factors previously discussed in the external market analysis section.

   Website: http://www.library.usyd.edu.au/databases/apais1.html

2. The Australian Business Index:

   This is a monthly index dealing with business-related articles from various newspapers and business periodicals. The articles are listed according to subject heading in alphabetical order.

3. Business Periodicals Index:

Again, a monthly issued index with articles alphabetically listed in a subject index. The periodicals are predominately United States publications. Therefore, the article content may not directly relate to Australian conditions and libraries and may not hold a number of the indexed periodicals. However, the articles may still be important and relevant because of the global nature of business and its associated information flow.

Web site: http://www.nla.gov.au/pathways/jnls/newsite/view/1125.html

4. Wilson's Business Periodicals Index:

Wilson's Business Periodicals Index provides information to track competitors, monitor new products, and gather data on industry and financial trends. The index provides indexing of over 500 key international English-language business periodicals including Business Week, Forbes, The Wall Street Journal, and The New York Times. There is a broad coverage of several key areas including accounting, acquisitions and mergers, advertising, banking, chemicals, engineering, finance and investments, government regulations, insurance, management, publishing, and taxation.

Website: http://www.ovid.com/site/catalog/DataBase/

• *Universities and Institutes of Technology*

A less obvious and yet no less relevant source of information for a small business is to examine any work, which may have been researched by tertiary students at universities and institutes of technology.

The Department of Industry, Technology and Commerce brings out a publication, containing a listing of small business research undertaken by tertiary students in Australia, and by small business associations. The publication is titled: "Register of Small Business Research, and is available from most university or institute libraries.

- *Private Research Organizations*

One such organization is the group which produces the Mintel Economic Management Report. This report is published four times each year and contains market analysis of various industries as well as a standard section on key economic indicators.

Since its inception, numerous volumes have been published with many industries analyzed. Fast food, overseas travel, furniture, chips and snacks, bread, auto accessories and microwave ovens are just some examples of those industries that Mintel has researched and reported on over the years.

Mintel Economic Management reports are available from academic libraries, and the information contained within can be relied on to be both accurate and relevant for decision making purposes.

Website: http://www.mintel.com/

KEEP IN MIND

Not all sources of secondary data are totally reliable. Sources such as the population census from the Australian Bureau of Statistics, Mintel reports and other government reports are among the most reliable.

Any information obtained from less recognized sources must be examined closely with a touch of healthy skepticism. In such cases, it is wise to ask yourself a few simple questions:

1. Who was it for? (Look at the source of and audience for the research)

2. Why is it available? (Examine any possible motives)

3. When was it done? (Is it still relevant for today?)

Using information from reliable sources is not always possible. Examine information for possible errors and always try to verify its findings.

3.2.2 PRIMARY INFORMATION

In many cases, the various sources of secondary information will sufficiently meet most business needs. In cases where those needs have not been adequately met by available secondary data sources, **primary information** is then required.

Primary information is data, which either does not already exist or perhaps is not available to you, and, therefore, needs to be collected specifically to fill a particular information need.

Primary information comes from market research activities, which can either be performed in-house or, by independent market research firms. Although recognized to be important, most small businesses generally cannot afford to outsource this activity. Consequently, this section of the book will take a thorough look at what is required when performing in-house research.

There are many types of data, which can be effectively, quickly and accurately obtained through surveys or questionnaires. Below is a list and explanation of the major data types:

- *Demographic Data*

This data literally "describes" people. Commonly used demographic variables form the basis for segmenting markets e.g. age, gender, stage in family lifecycle (ages of the respective adults and children in families), family size, marital status, country of birth, first spoken language, religion, residential area.

- *Socioeconomic Data*

This data refers to the standing that individuals have in a community There are four, interdependent variables that can be used to determine not only the levels of disposable income, but also likely spending patterns of the people being surveyed. They are education, occupation, income and social beliefs.

- *Attitudinal Data*

This data refers to the attitudes, beliefs, ideas and convictions, which your customers hold in relation to something e.g. a product, a particular brand, a product feature.

- *Awareness Data*

This data refers to what customers know about a certain product or brand e.g., the advertising of a product. Low customer knowledge and awareness of a product will usually contribute to poor product sales.

- *Intention Data*

This data refers to anticipated and planned future customer behavior with respect to purchases of a particular product or product line. For example, do customers not already buying your product intend to start buying it? Or, if they are already buying it, do they intend to keep buying at the same levels?

- *Motivation Data*

This data relates to those factors, which motivate a person to buy (or perhaps not to buy) a particular product offering. These motivating factors are generally considered hard to isolate for two main reasons. First, many people do not know what has motivated them and secondly, some people lie. Examples of motivating factors include price, product image, color range, warranty, loyalty to a brand name, strong advertising, social acceptance.

- *Behavioral Data*

This data refers to what people have been doing, are doing or will be doing with regards to purchasing. Here, you discover more about the purchaser and the user. (Note: the purchaser and the user are not always one and the same). The sorts of questions to ask here include what is bought (i.e. actual vs. perceived attributes), where and when do they buy, how do they buy, who buys it.

Developing a Questionnaire

Having now examined the various types of data that can be obtained using a questionnaire or survey, the next step for the small business is to design an appropriate questionnaire. The questionnaire should be based on gaps from the secondary information.

Outlined below is a simple, step-by-step model, which can be used by any small business to design a question-naire.

Step 1: Review information requirements, to isolate precisely what information the business needs to collect, that is not found from secondary sources.

Step 2: Develop a list of potential questions to obtain the required information.

Step 3: Evaluate each potential question on the following grounds:

a. Will your target market understand it?

b. Are the questions unbiased and are all possible answers accounted for?

c. Is the respondent qualified to answer all questions? For example, a single man cannot complete a questionnaire on marriage.

d. Will they answer it? Remove any insecurity from the respondent e.g., fear of any part of their responses becoming publicly known.

Step 4: Decide on the exact wording of each question. Keep in mind exactly who your target market is.

Step 5: Test the final draft of the questionnaire. The questionnaire must first be pre-tested with subjects who are themselves part of your target market. For example, if your target market comprises women who are 30 and over, working in a professional capacity, the question-naire cannot be pre-tested with stay-at-home mothers.

Step 6: Examine whether the information obtained was exactly the information you required for each question. If yes, the question can be placed into the official ques-tionnaire. If no, re-write question(s) based on errors found during pre-testing. Retest new questions within the appropriate target market if time permits.

Step 7: Give the questionnaire to your target market and accurately record survey results for market analysis and planning.

It's simple really. When in doubt, ask.

Sample Questionnaire

The following example is a sample questionnaire for a small retail business in a suburban shopping center, which specializes in selling televisions and videos. On the sale of each unit, the purchaser is asked to complete the questionnaire, on the understanding that the information is for the benefit of the retailer and confidential. A small cash refund is offered as an incentive to promote a higher response rate. Note that this sample questionnaire does not represent the only way or the best way, but rather one particular way to obtain certain information needed by the business.

ASGARD'S TELEVISION AND DVD-VIDEO STORE QUESTIONNARE
(Business Identification)

To improve future service levels and
product management

(Questionnaire objective)

Purchaser's Name: _____

Address: _____

_____P/C_____

Phone_____

Gender of Purchaser: ❏ Male   ❏ Female

Age of Purchaser, are you...

❑ Under 18 years

❑ 18-30 years

❑ 31-40 years

❑ 41-50 years

❑ 51-60 years

❑ 61-70 years

❑ Over 70 years

Do you:

❑ Rent your home

❑ Own your home

❑ Other (please specify):

_____

What is your annual family income?

❑ Under $40,000

❑ $40,000-$60,000

❑ $60,000-$80,000

❑ $80,000-$100,000

❑ Above $100,000

Check the item you bought

❑ TV

❑ Video

❑ DVD

❑ Other (please specify)

_____

Brand Name:

_____

Model:

_____

Purchased Date:

_____ /_____ / _____

Reason for product purchase:

❑ For yourself to replace existing unit

❑ For yourself to add to existing unit(s)

❑ For yourself as initial purchase of this unit type

❑ As a present for someone else

Which room in your home will the unit be placed?

❑ Living Room

❑ Dining Room

❑ Bedroom

❑ Kitchen

❑ Other (please specify)

_____

Which of the following best describes your household?

❑ A single person

❑ Couple – no children

❑ Couple with all children < 6 years old

❑ Couple with children 6-18 years old

❑ Couple with dependent children >18

❑ Other (please specify)

_____

What initially motivated you to buy this unit?

❑ Advertising

(Please specify what type)

_____

❑ Friend's recommendation

❑ Salesperson's advice

❑ Store demonstration

❑ Read in magazine (please specify which one if possible)

_____

Was this your initial choice?

❑ Yes   ❑ No

Why did you finally decide to buy this unit?

❑ Unit price

❑ Guarantee

❑ Unit features and accessories

❑ Brand Reputation

❑ Unit design and overall look

❑ Previous experience and satisfaction with the same brand

❑ Other (please specify)

_____

What was the main reason for choosing our store?

❑ Product range

❑ Price levels

❑ Store location

❑ Persuasive advertising

❑ Friendly staff

❑ Favorable past experi-
ences

How satisfied are you with
the unit so far?

❑ Totally satisfied

❑ Mostly satisfied

❑ Too early to tell

❑ Mostly dissatisfied

❑ Totally dissatisfied

❑ Reasons for satisfaction
or dissatisfaction:

_____

_____

Any further comments on
any aspect of the product
or our shop are most wel-
comed:

_____

_____

	Pre-paid postage
Business Manager
Business Name
Business address	

Fold
Here

- -

Sender's Name and Address

_____

_____
_____

_____

Fold
here

- -

(Space here to promote the incentive for answering
the questionnaire)

Fig 3.3: Example
of a Self Enclosed
Mail Questionnaire

Alternative Survey Methods

Having by this stage designed an appropriate question-naire for your business, based on the information gaps which were not filled through secondary sources, the next step is to decide on which survey method to use.

Let us examine three survey methods, outlining the relative advantages and disadvantages of each.

* *Telephone Interviewing*

  Advantages:

  1. Fairly inexpensive per response.
  2. Can be done using computer aided systems.
  3. Good for when respondents are scattered over an extensive, geographic area.
  4. Non-threatening to respondent who is in the safety of his/her own home.
  5. Possibility to clarify questions.
  6. Nearly everyone has a phone (approximately 95% of people).
  7. High response rate usually.
  8. Quick to do.

  Disadvantages:

  1. Only a limited number of questions can be asked (due to the conventional maximum of 10 minutes per interview).
  2. Only possible when the phone number of respon-dent is available.

3. Unsuitable method for when respondents need to see the product.

4. Only fairly simple questions can be asked.

5. Can be seen as intrusive.

- *Mail Questionnaire*

With mail questionnaires, it is vital to include a good cover letter at the start of the questionnaire. This letter will explain the reason you are sending the questionnaire and more importantly from the respondent's viewpoint, "what's in it for him/her." Most people need to be able to rationalize to themselves, exactly why they should bother. Perhaps the offer of a small, but effective token on completion of the questionnaire, such as a lottery ticket, will produce the required incentive. Clearly the information is not for free, but the results that come from good research more than justify the expense to the business.

Advantages:

1. Can ask more complex questions (compared to the phone).

2. Useful for widely scattered respondent population.

3. Fairly low cost (especially on national basis).

4. Easy to conduct.

5. Not intrusive.

Disadvantages:

1. Incomplete questionnaires.

2. Low response rate could make this method costly.

3. No probing possible.

4. Cannot observe respondents (did the respondent or someone else complete it?).

5. Slow return rate.

6. Only possible when we know respondents' addresses.

- *Personal Interviews*

In an ideal world this method is perhaps the best for the majority of small business especially those involved in retail. Wherever possible, it should be used.

Advantages:

1. Suitable when long, detailed questionnaires are involved.

2. Leads to a high response rate, as people in general prefer to talk rather than write.

3. Good for obtaining information on beliefs, attitudes, knowledge etc.

4. Can use product display (visual element possible).

5. Greater chance to probe.

6. More questions can be asked (compared to the phone).

7. You can ensure that the respondents fully understand what is being asked.

Disadvantages:

1. Expensive if you have to travel to their homes,

2. May be threatened by your presence and, therefore, may lead to false answers.

3.3   SWOT ANALYSIS

The analysis of strengths and weaknesses, opportunities and threats (SWOT) comes out of the internal business and external market analyses. The better the latter analyses, the stronger the outcomes of the SWOT analysis.

A SWOT analysis will qualify the internal strengths and weaknesses of a business. Moreover, it identifies the possible opportunities and threats the business will face in the short and longer term. Unlike the internal strengths and weaknesses, which are all controllable, the external opportunities and threats are uncontrollable by the business.

Strengths and weaknesses should be listed relative to your rival businesses. For example, if you have cash reserves of $10,000 (which is undoubtedly an asset), you may regard it as a strength.

If, however, all your key rivals have at least $50,000 cash reserves, your $10,000 is in fact, a relative weakness.

3.3.1   INDICATED ACTIONS

Each point listed in the SWOT analysis will almost certainly have some desired action linked to it that should be performed or at least be considered by the business. Each of these desired responses is called an INDICATED ACTION.

In the case of the small business with a relatively modest cash reserve, it may not be possible to take advantage of upcoming opportunities. Therefore, the indicated action for this business would be to investigate and arrange for an appropriate line of credit (or equity loan). You must know exactly how much additional capital you can borrow, and know when, from whom, over what time frame and at what interest rate, etc.

It is not enough to know you do not have enough liquidity; you need to act to take control of the situation.

3.3.2 RESOURCES

Once appropriate indicated actions are formulated, it is important to decide on the level of resources required to carry out each indicated action. Again, using the example of the business requiring additional access to cash, different types of resources will be needed to negotiate this.

To begin with there is the obvious financial resource (cost) in the form of an establishment fee which financial institutions typically charge when creating new business loans. Moreover, in the longer term, these borrowings will require additional funds to be paid off.

From the point of view of non-financial resources the most precious resource is time, i.e. someone from the business will need to prepare the appropriate documentation that the banks will require.

3.3.3 OPPORTUNITY COST

The final aspect of a thorough SWOT analysis is to include any thoughts on **Opportunity Cost**. Put simply, Opportunity Cost is the cost of not implementing the next best alternative. For example, if you are thinking of spending money in one area, the idea of Opportunity Cost challenges you to think about where else that money could be spent, possibly with a better result.

It is possibly the least understood cost, and yet potentially can give great insight into how valid (or not) your contemplated actions are. Opportunity Cost forces you to consider alternative actions as well as the proposed action.

Using the ongoing example of the business needing to organize a line of credit, the opportunity cost could be as follows. In addition to approaching a bank, the business owner may consider other ways of generating the cash e.g., selling off excess equipment or surplus assets or perhaps redirecting a portion of projected profit, previously earmarked for another use.

In this instance, given the relatively low cost of choosing the original bank option, it is likely that the alternatives would not be viable. In other words, the opportunity cost of not implementing the next best alternative is low and, therefore, the original action is likely to be carried out.

On the next page is a summary of this example, as it would appear in a SWOT analysis.

S/W/O/T	Implication	Indicated Action	Resources	Opportunity Cost
Strength: High individual skill level of employees.	Retention of quality skilled staff members.	Incentives for employees to maintain motivation levels.	Funding of incentive program.	Divert incentive funding to other capital expenditure.
Weakness: Lacking cash reserves when compared to key rivals.	Decreased ability to quickly respond to opportunities and changing conditions, which require prompt cash outlays.	Organize relevant documentation and arrange interviews with preferred financial institution to discuss the business needs with regards to an equity loan.	Financial and human resources to facilitate the specifics.	Redirect some income to this function or conduct a partial sell-off of any buffer stock or surplus assets to increase cash reserve.
Opportunity: Two rivals closing down in the new year.	Potential to gain customer base from these rival businesses.	Incentives for rivals to direct business your way.	Funding allocation to cater for customer base expansion.	Use resources to fund other areas of more immediate need.
Threat: Major new rival business opening in the new year in the area.	Potential for lost business as customers are attracted to this market leader.	Gather market research to uncover why customers might be attracted to this rival and whether you are meeting your customers' needs, based on your current marketing activities.	Funding and time to confirm market needs and to conduct competitor analysis.	Continue to support marketing activities at the current level, without any regard to the potential impact from the new rival.

DECISION:

- Strengths: Fund and organize incentive program to help retain key staff.

- Weaknesses: Organize for a line of credit to improve access to available funds.

- Opportunities: Leverage the closing of rival firms to expand customer base.

- Threats: Gather intelligence of new rival and design a marketing plan to counter.

After completing an initial analysis (including both an internal and external analysis) for your business and incorporating market information from secondary sources (and possibly, primary sources), capture the key findings on the SWOT analysis template. The SWOT analysis needs to be done and reviewed at least quarterly, to ensure that it remains current and reflective of what is relevant today and tomorrow, and not yesterday.

S/W/O/T Analysis Template	Implication	Indicated Action	Resources	Opportunity Cost
STRENGTHS				

WEAKNESSES				
OPPORTUNITIES				
THREATS				

3.4   MARKET SEGMENTATION

Market segmentation refers to the process of dividing a market into segments of customers with similar needs for eventual targeting. A targeted market approach will aim to satisfy the needs of individual groups within the overall market, through different marketing strategies.

On the other hand, a **mass marketing** approach assumes that everyone in the market has the same needs. Therefore, the same marketing strategy is adopted for everyone.

EXAMPLE

Two shoe stores open recently within the same retail shopping mall.

The marketing savvy owner of the first store, after analysis of the shoe market, decides to target a specific market segment, i.e., athletic footwear. This owner has found a niche that is both growing in size and economically viable.

In contrast, the second shoe store owner, who has little understanding of market segmentation, opens a store that offers a broad range of shoes for men, women and children. This in a mall that already has four other existing shoe stores.

The former has aimed specifically at meeting the needs of a particular group. The latter, however, has no clear product differentiation in an environment of intense existing competition.

In the absence of a **Unique Product Offering** (U.P.O.), every attempt should be made to capture a viable segment of the market from the mass-marketer. This is important because customers do not just buy your product (e.g. sports shoes), they also buy your specialized knowledge and experience in this area.

Let us examine the book selling market and how it can be segmented.

Task 1: Segment Market into subgroups

1. Academic/Reference books

2. Religion / Spirituality books

3. Detective/Crime stories & Mystery thrillers

4. Comic books, Fantasy and Science fiction

5. Biographies

6. Australiana

7. Humour

8. Children's books, Fairy tales, Children's fiction, and Tiny tots

9. Cookbooks

10. Fishing books

11. Photography books

12. Gardening books

13. Animals/Nature books

14. Crafts and Lifestyles

15. Modern Literature and Classics

16. Poetry, Plays and Drama

17. Fine Arts and Antiques.

18. Travel books

19. Psychic and Occult books

20. Music and the Performing Arts (Television, Film, Theatre, Radio)

21. General Fiction

22. Sports, Games, Hobbies and Games books

23. Military

24. Planes, Trains, Automobiles

25. Current Affairs

26. Health and Beauty, Self-Improvement, Medical and Childcare books

27. Braille books

28. Talking books

Task 2: Examine each segment to highlight the ones that present the greatest market potential, both in the short and long term, given your business resources, competitive climate and current market conditions.

Task 3: Select the most appropriate target segments, based on your ability to meet the needs of that group. Use the matching process (see section 3.5) and formulate marketing strategies and plans to effectively meet their needs.

3.4.1 POSSIBLE DIMENSIONS FOR MARKET SEGMENTATIONS

Each business will need to segment its market. The various dimensions for segmenting markets can be categorized into two areas:

- Customer descriptive dimensions, and

- Customer behavioral dimensions.

The former refers to those dimensions that help the business "draw a picture" and accurately describe who the customers are (i.e. demographics, location information, psychographics and socioeconomics). The latter answers broad questions such as what the customers are buying and why they are buying these products.

Customer Descriptive Dimensions

- *Demographics*

  Age: Infant under 1 year, 1-5, 6-12, 3-17, 8-25, 26-35, 36-45, 46-55, 56-65, over 65.

  Gender of Person: female or male.

  *Stage in family lifecycle: bachelor stage, young singles not living at home, younger couples with no children, full nest 1st stage: young married, youngest child under six, full nest 2nd stage: young married, youngest child over six, full nest 3rd stage: older couples with at least one child still at home, empty nest 1st stage: older couples with no children at home, separated or divorced. *(*Source - adapted from the works of W.D. Wells and Gr. Gubar, "Life Cycle Concept in Marketing Research", Journal of Marketing Research, 3/11/66, pg.362, August 1968 pg. 267).*

  Marital Status: single and never married, married, separated, divorced.

  Household size: 1 – 2 people, 3 – 4 people, 5 – 6 people, > 6 people.

  Birthplace: Africa, Australia, Great Britain, Canada, China, Germany, Greece, Holland, India, Indonesia, Italy, Japan, Lebanon, Mexico, Middle East, New Zealand, Scandinavia, America, South America, Spain, Vietnam, Korea, Russia, Croatia, Other European, Other Asian, Other.

  First spoken language: English, French, German, Spanish, Greek, Italian, Serbian/Croatian, Vietnamese, Korean, Japanese, Cantonese, Mandarin, Other.

Religion: Anglican, Baptist, Catholic, Greek Orthodox, Jewish, Muslim, Christian, Other, No religious following.

- *Location*

By state/territory: Australian Capital Territory, New South Wales, Northern Territory, Queensland, South Australia, Tasmania, Victoria, Western Australia.

By Statistical Local Areas: according to the A.B.S. key census regional breakdown.

By Statistical Retail Areas: according to the A.B.S. key census regional breakdown.

By quantifying the size of the State, City, Local Area, Retail Area in terms of the number of people: Under 5,000; 5,000 – 20,000; 20,000 – 50,000; 50,001 – 75,000; 75,001 – 100,000.

- *Socioeconomic*

Education   -Primary school graduate or less.

-Some high school, but not graduate.

-High school graduate.

-Some tertiary level study, but not graduate.

-Tertiary qualification (degree or diploma).

-Higher degree (Master's, PhD).

-Trade qualification.

-Other.

Occupation   -Management and upper administration.

-Professional careers.

-Semi-professionals.

-Clerical.

-Trades people.

-Salespeople.

-Machinists.

-Unskilled labor.

-Other.

Annual Income

-Nil	$1-$4,000	$4,001-$8,000	$8,001-$16,000	$16,001-$18,000
$18,001-$24,000	$24,001-$30,000	$30,001-$36,000	$36,001-$44,000	$44,001-$52,000
$52,001-$64,000	$64,001-$80,000	$80,001-$100,000	over $100,000	

Media Habit: newspaper, television, radio, Internet surfer.

- *Psychology*

  Personality: easy going/laid back, competitive, quiet, talkative, etc.

  Attitudinal: refers to beliefs, ideas, and convictions that the customer holds (e.g. for or against the pill as a form of contraception).

Values: values include the moral and ethical standards a person lives by. (e.g. honesty, mutual respect, social awareness and responsibility, materialism)

Lifestyle: active versus inactive, social versus non-social, environmentally conscious or not.

Interests: pastimes, recreational activities, hobbies.

Customer self-image: modern thinker/liberal, old-fashioned/conservative, intellectual/cultured.

Customer Behavioral Dimensions

What does the customer buy, when, how and why?

Product type:

- **Convenience goods** (staple or emergency) e.g. ice cream, biscuits etc.

- **Shopping goods** that are homogenous (similar products with little differentiation such as gasoline) or heterogeneous (products that are easily distinguished from rival brands on some meaningful basis e.g. computer software packages).

- **Specialty goods** e.g. laser printer paper.

- **Unsought goods** e.g. encyclopedias.

Current User Status: User, non-user.

Times of Purchase: Weekday, weekend, morning, afternoon, evening, etc.

Usage rate: Daily, weekly, every two weeks, monthly, annually, occasionally, never.

Purchase pattern: On a regular basis, irregular basis, other.

Product attributes:

- Physical - e.g. product size, taste, shape, color, packaging, etc. (N.B. These attributes account for the logical reasons for purchasing a product.)

- Perceived - e.g. sex appeal (as gained by a perfume), masculinity (as gained by a certain cigarette). (N.B. These perceived attributes account for the emotional (sometimes irrational) reasons for product purchase.)

  Often a purchase is made because of a combination of both types of attributes.

User Benefits: User benefits derived from the product attributes and specific to the product.

Motivational factors: Both real and perceived by the consumer. This can be a blend of anything from protection, comfort and freedom to status, quality and image. Ultimately, it is the satisfaction derived by customers from the product benefits that motivate the consumer to purchase the product.

Customer loyalty: strong, moderate, low, none.

Reasons to Purchase:

- Logical, relate to actual attributes within product e.g. twin blade for closer shave.

- Relate to perceived attributes e.g. increased social acceptance by wearing a particular brand of sunglasses.

3.4.2 SELECTING THE BEST DIMENSION FOR SEGMENTING YOUR MARKET

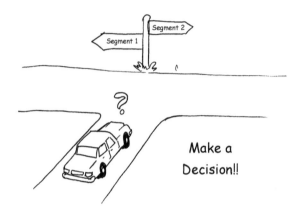

Most markets can be segmented in a multitude of ways. The question is what is the best way to segment a particular market? Although there is no definite answer to this question, the segment(s) that can be supported resource-wise will become the obvious choice(s).

3.4.3 CRITERIA FOR EVALUATING MARKET SEGMENTS

Once a business has performed market segmentation, it is time to critically evaluate each of the segments according to the potential for profitability.

The criteria most commonly used to evaluate whether or not to target selected market segments are:

1. Ability to be quantified - A market segment must be quantifiable, e.g., what is the potential number of customers? How much are they willing to spend?

2. Ability to identify groups with similar needs - For market segmentation and subsequent target

marketing to be done successfully, it is vital that you are able to identify and group together people with similar needs that the business can fulfill.

NOTE: These needs can be based on product usage, product attributes, location of business, benefits sought by customer or on any other appropriate dimension.

3. Actual size - A market segment must be big enough, e.g., are there enough customers? Do they have enough money to spend?

4. Ability to communicate with the segment - With few exceptions, most market segments can be reached on both a promotional and distribution level. The critical factor is whether the net cost to achieve and sustain this communication is within acceptable levels, so that your business can effectively communicate with this segment.

Need to Combine Multiple Criteria to Gain Accuracy and Insight

Marketers have perennially flagged this potential when they speak of the need to consider both demographic and psychographic criteria in market segmentation.

Consider a situation where some market research is being proposed to 40 to 45 year old males, working in middle management group. The aim of the research is to determine the size of this particular market segment and also to determine whether there would be increased spending by this group in the next three years; and if so, on what.

If these were to be the only criteria used, you may get a result that is unreliable because the criteria used are too broad.

To obtain more meaningful results, this group can be further segmented into two groups e.g. married men with children or who expect to have children within the next two years versus those who are either married without children or single and in both cases, have no intention of having children.

These two groups although similar demographically, are significantly different in terms of what their future spending is likely to be. Only when you include these additional criteria are you able to differentiate between the two market segments and the specific areas of future spending for both groups.

From this more detailed breakdown your business would then be able to assess the viability of these separate market segments, as a basis for further decision-making.

3.5   THE MATCHING PROCESS

Once the market has been segmented, a matching process is conducted using the Segmentation Analysis Grid. The Grid examines both currently targeted segments and the viability of potential segments.

The Segmentation Analysis Grid also highlights **Key Success Factors** (KSFs). These KSFs are those factors that are essential in delivering the required product to a target customer group to consistently satisfy their unmet needs.

Here is an example of how you might utilize the Grid:

(Segmentation Analysis Grid Template)	Currently targeted segment	Prospective segment
Market Segments	Broad shoe market – children, men and women	Upmarket male shoe market
Specific Unmet Needs of Customer	Moderately priced and quality shoes	Better quality more stylish, more comfortable, more durable shoes
Product to Meet Needs of Customer	Middle market brands	Upmarket brands known to have superior quality and style
Key Benefits Derived by Customer	Reasonably comfortable shoes at a reasonable price	Satisfaction and status
Key Success Factors	Full range of colors, styles and sizes	Access to European and other international suppliers

The matching process matches the business strengths and weaknesses (from the SWOT analysis) to these KSFs, with the aim of identifying the market segments with the greatest potential for the business.

Using the shoe shop example above, the SWOT analysis conducted by this business could potentially have indicated that the store is located in an upmarket boutique shopping center that has a number of exclusive menswear shops. Given this strength, the owner of the business may, after further research, conclude that targeting the prospective segment could well be more lucrative than persisting with the current broad segment.

Here is a template that you can use for your business:

(Segmentation Analysis Grid Template)	Currently targeted	Prospective segments
Market Segments		
Specific Unmet Needs of Customer		
Product to Meet Needs of Customer		
Key Benefits Derived by Customer		
Key Success Factors		

3.6   SELECTING MARKET SEGMENTS TO BE TARGETED

Regardless of how many market segments emerge or how well defined they are, you must still decide which (if any) of the viable segments should be targeted.

In some situations segmentation may reveal both small and large market niches, which are not currently being adequately serviced. This means that there is no business actively targeting these niches so the needs of these groups remain unmet.

Once 'discovered', the larger niches often go on to attract more and larger rivals. Whereas, the smaller niches may not be attractive because they have a much smaller profit potential and, therefore, represent real and sustainable opportunities for small businesses that are able to service them in a more personal way and develop customer loyalty.

Therefore, when deciding which segments to target for your business, don't just look at the absolute dollar size of the segment. Although it remains an important factor, it is not the only consideration. Think more in terms of how your business would operate in this area given current and potential competitors.

Taking a long term view will ensure the sustainability of your business.

3.6.1 WRITING A CUSTOMER PROFILE FOR YOUR SELECTED TARGET MARKET

Once you have selected your target market, it is useful to write a half to one page customer profile (see example below). Imagine the typical man, woman or child from your target group and write down everything you think you know about them. This knowledge will come from various sources ranging from personal experience with these customers through to market research.

This activity can be used as a precursor to writing the marketing blueprint, to ensure that your marketing strategies align with this broad profile of the customer.

CUSTOMER PROFILE

'Theo' is a 16 year old student and attends high school or university. He is a great fan of science fiction and enjoys reading comics, which he has done for most of his life. Many of his friends also enjoy comics; they enjoy reading them and discussing them. Theo also enjoys movies about his favorite comic characters, as well as science fiction films.

Because Theo is still at school/university, he does not have a lot of discretionary income. He does not drive a car and, therefore, relies on public transportation to get around, as do his friends. Given that school/university dominates his weekdays, he does his shopping later in the day or on weekends.

Theo is an avid listener of modern music including rap and hard rock. He is a football fan and loves being a sports spectator on the weekends. He also plays basketball.

From the customer profile on the previous page, several key insights can be inferred. Some key points include:

- The majority of comic readers are young males aged 10 to 25 (this both defines the market and also raises interesting possibilities to expand the market later on to females).

- The connection between comics and other related science fiction media and paraphernalia.

- The cost sensitive nature of the market, given other existing rival stores and the generally low levels of discretionary income these students have.

- The need to have the store in an area that is both central and close to public transportation given that many from the target customer group do not drive.

- The need to be open for extended hours both on weekday evenings and weekends given the commitments that the group have to both academic studies and weekend activities such as sporting events and team participation.

- Preference for parking facilities if customers are given transportation by a parent/friend.

- Implications for cross promoting the store with other popular promotional media such as the key radio station that specialises in the popular music most enjoyed by the target group.

This list is by no means exhaustive, but rather demonstrates how effective this approach can be for any small business when making additional connections with individual pieces of information you already have. This in turn can be used to strengthen your marketing strategy and ensure that all proposed plans are accurately aligned to the real world needs of the target customer group.

SUMMARY

- You must make full use of all available primary and secondary sources of market information.

- Secondary information sources relate to existing sources of information, which can either be internally or externally collected.

- Primary information sources relate to data that do not currently exist, but is obtained through various forms of research.

- In designing an effective questionnaire, you must first determine the information requirements, design the appropriate questions and pre-test the finished form on its target market.

- Approaches to surveying include telephone interviews, direct mail and personal interviews.

- The SWOT analysis looks at both the controllable strengths and weaknesses of the business, and the uncontrollable opportunities and threats that currently exist within the market place.

- The market can be broken down into smaller segments comprising populations of similar needs.

- The matching process matches key success factors to each market segment, and together with the SWOT analysis results, identifies segments with the greatest business potential

- By writing a thorough customer profile you will have a better understanding of the needs of your target customer group

CHAPTER 4

STAGE B: ESTABLISHING EFFECTIVE BUSINESS OBJECTIVES

Every business regardless of size, product offering, location or sales turnover, needs to have a set of effective business objectives if it is to grow and perform well into the future. Few small businesses realize the importance of formulating business objectives due to (in many cases) a false sense of security arising from success in the initial stages of the business.

It is not surprising then that so many small businesses after an initial period of success start to suffer badly due to this lack of direction, especially when successful rivals have set good objectives and subsequently formulated strategies designed to achieve those predetermined objectives.

It is not enough to have a rough idea or notion as to the preferred direction of your business. These objectives must be both specific and clear. Tedious though it may sound, they must always be written down. A written document allows for your thoughts to be crystallized, enforces a sense of commitment and forms a historical document as your business evolves and as your objectives inevitably change.

This chapter will deal entirely with the subject of establishing sound and effective business objectives and includes a discussion of the various categories of objectives.

A set of criteria will also be provided to evaluate the overall effectiveness of any current or future business objectives. A case study will also be discussed in which goal setting will be viewed specifically from a small business perspective.

4.1   THE HIERARCHY OF BUSINESS OBJECTIVES

There are both operational and marketing objectives to consider.

4.1.1 OPERATIONAL OBJECTIVES

The operational objectives relate to the administrative side of things. These objectives focus on the mechanics of the business and can also be thought of as the "non marketing" goal setting section. The operational objectives include:

- *Financial Objectives*

These objectives, as the name suggests, encompass all areas of financial planning. Here a small business draws up budgets for the year based on both past experience and current requirements.

These budgets will make projections for all financial areas of the business e.g. sales figures, cost figures (including cost of sales, operating expenses and non-operating expenses), overall profitability (before and after tax), and any other appropriate financial projections.

- *Personnel Objectives*

These objectives relate to the management of human resources for the small business. Here the business examines and determines both its current and future personnel needs. If, for example, your business is growing, then it is likely that extra personnel may have to be recruited later in the year. Based on such projected growth, the business would need to anticipate these future needs and have suitably qualified people chosen, trained and waiting.

In another example, the computer systems may need updating in the near future. In this case, the business owner may need to organize training for the staff.

- *Production Objectives*

Production objectives are applicable to those small businesses that manufacture (in whole or in part) their product offerings. Projections of units produced and the level of raw materials required are anticipated. It should be noted that these production objectives would need to be determined prior to the formulating of financial objectives.

4.1.2 MARKETING OBJECTIVES

Marketing objectives involve not only setting goals about the people you want to attract to your business, but also setting objectives about the controllable variables of the marketing mix. Moreover, the business must aim at achieving a certain share of the market, given its relative strengths and weaknesses.

- *Target Market Objectives*

  Here the business makes a decision on which particular segment(s) of customers to target.

- *Marketing Mix Objectives*

  The **marketing mix** is the combination of the four main factors (i.e. product, price, promotion and place) which the business controls to best meet the needs of the targeted customers. Objectives, therefore, need to be formulated for each of these four factors.

Product Objectives: These are the objectives which cover all areas relating to the products or product lines, and may include the following:

- Exactly which products (existing and/or new) are being offered to the target markets.
- Benefits provided and need(s) they satisfy.
- Brands sold for each product category.
- Availability of after sales service.
- Guarantees (if any) being offered for each product or service.
- Any additional services.
- Products to be manufactured by the business and products to be bought.
- Operating hours of the business.

- Terms of payment.

Price Objectives: These objectives deal with all matters relating to pricing considerations, and may include the following considerations:

- Which of the three main pricing policies will be adopted (i.e. **skimming, penetration or market pricing policy)?**

- What pricing levels will be adopted for each product?

- Will these pricing levels vary as the product moves through the product life cycle and if so, how and when?

- What discounts and/or allowances will be offered to which people, under what conditions and when?

Promotion Objectives: These objectives should include all activities that aim to positively influence the buying behavior of your target market. Promotional objectives must do more than raise the awareness of your business and its products. Promotion is the communication with the target market that convinces the customers that their needs are best met by your business rather than someone else's. Promotion can be directed not only at customers, but also at your staff.

Separate goals (when? how? how much?) should be set for each promotional method used. Promotional methods include:

- Sales promotion
- Personal selling
- Advertising

- Publicity

Place: These objectives relate not only to the location of your business, but also the distribution network that exists. It includes everything from product manufacture to point of purchase outlet. Any proposed changes to the business location or current distribution channels are included here.

- *Sales/Market Share Objectives*

The business examines its current **market share**, i.e., what percentage of the total market (either in dollars or units sold) it holds. Based on this and overall market trends, a projected market share objective is set for the next financial period.

An aim to increase market share must be accompanied by a specific strategy. For example, a strategic lowering of product price may lead to an increase in market share. There must always be a sound rationale behind each objective, without which any attempt to achieve the objective is unlikely to succeed.

For most small businesses, the market share held can be relatively small and expressed as a share of the local market, not a statewide or national market share.

4.2   CRITERIA FOR MEASURING THE EFFECTIVENESS OF BUSINESS OBJECTIVES

Having examined the hierarchy of business objectives, the next step for a small business is to establish a list of criteria to evaluate if the objectives are appropriate and effective.

Criteria #1:   Objectives should always be quantifiable i.e. they need to be measurable. Otherwise it is impossible to determine if they have been met or not. For example, "Profits to increase" is not a valid objective, as it does not state by how much. However, "Profits to increase by 10 % over last year's" is quantifiable.

Criteria #2:   Objectives must always stipulate a time frame or date by which the objective needs to be accomplished e.g. increase by 10% in 12 months.

Criteria #3:   Objectives must always be clear and specific in nature, never general e.g. "objective to improve performance" is not specific, as we do not have any further details.

Criteria #4:   Objectives must be based on the results of your market analysis.

Criteria #5:   Objectives should cover all relevant areas of your business.

Criteria #6:   Each objective should be congruent and not clash with the other objectives e.g., unit market share increase with price decreases.

Criteria #7:   Objectives must always be reasonable; although challenging, but should still be attainable. It is useless to aim for a 100% growth each year. Similarly, you are doing yourself a disservice by being too conservative when projecting a low growth scenario in an aggressively growing market. Ultimately, you need to be bold, but at the same time, realistic.

Note that this list is not exhaustive. It is a guideline to gauge the overall suitability of your business objectives. There are no absolute rights or wrongs in goal setting.

4.3   CASE STUDY HIGHLIGHTING THE BUSINESS OBJECTIVES OF A TYPICAL SMALL BUSINESS

Setting the scene:

Crusty's Hot Bread and Cake Shop:

* overproduces certain products.

* does not offer a number of products that are being requested by customers, but are sold by competitors.

* has an experienced staff member due to take maternity leave later in the year.

* operates for fewer hours than other hot bread stores in the area.

Six other rivals in the area have closed down in the last six years. Comparisons have revealed that Crusty's prices are slightly lower than other local stores across the main product lines.

Market Analysis:

Number of stores making up local market: 12

Average weekly trading hours per store: 48 hours

Total number of employees in these stores: 49

Average number of employees per store: 4

Total turnover for all stores: $1,448,000 last year

Average turnover per store: $ 75,167 last year

Analysis of Crusty's Bread and Cake Shop for last year:

Average weekly trading hours: 44 hours

Turnover: $150,000

Market share held by shop: $150,000/$1,448,000
                               =10%

The market has grown from $1,353,000 to $1,448,000 in the last six years. This represents a growth of $95,000 (7% i.e. 95,000/1,353,000). Therefore, the average growth per year over the last six years is 1.16% (i.e. 7/6). However, the average turnover per store has increased by 10% per year per store, due to having six less stores, compared to six years earlier. Assuming that further stores do not close down, and the slow rate of market growth continues, (i.e. 1% per year), each store's turnover would only marginally increase by the same amount (i.e. 1%).

Based on the above analysis of both the overall local market and the small business in question, the business is now in a position to formulate appropriate business objectives.

4.3.1 CASE STUDY - OPERATIONAL OBJECTIVES

(i) Financial

Based on the above analysis, the business will aim to generate sales in the next financial period of $160,000 (from $150,000) representing a 6% increase in sales due to overall business improvements. Costs should increase by approximately 3%, due to the extra operating hours planned, to increase hours in line with the other local stores. This should ensure that currently unsold stock at the end of each day will be sold, but an additional 5% production is envisaged due to new products being made available.

(ii) Personnel

Current staff levels are believed to be adequate even given the projected 20% increase in turnover. However, one staff member coming up for maternity leave, will need to be replaced for twelve months later this year. Arrangements should, therefore, be made to organize and train a suitable replacement.

(iii) Production

A production increase of 5% on current production levels is planned for the year. This should increase over-all sales by 6%. In-house research has revealed certain breads not currently being offered in the shop, will be in demand and, therefore, will be produced. Conversely, currently overstocked breads will be produced in much smaller amounts. This should ensure a more profitable mix of products.

4.3.2 CASE STUDY - MARKETING OBJECTIVES

(i) Target market

After effectively segmenting the market, it was found that the most obvious segment in the area is based on religious and cultural grounds, as there is a large Jewish population. Therefore, the business can target the local Jewish community and develop its marketing mix strategies accordingly.

(ii) Marketing mix

- **Product:** existing product lines will be modified given the survey results. Some slow selling products already available will either be produced in smaller amounts or not at all, and some products not currently available, will be introduced to meet expressed customer needs e.g. pita bread, etc.

- **Price:** the business will continue to sell its products marginally below the price of its main competitors. This will be done for two reasons:

  This market involves a product line, which is basically homogeneous (the same) in all shops. Consequently, it is a very price sensitive market. In this case, raising the prices would probably mean a loss of market share.

  Having the price slightly below the main competitors is a way of differentiating Crusty's shop from the others in a market where the actual product offering cannot be easily differentiated. Therefore, it is advantageous to differentiate on a price-basis and promote that advantage wherever possible e.g. on the carry bags.

- **Promotion:** the business will promote itself to enhance its image of quality and price in the following ways:

- Flyers on shop counter promoting the prices and products offered.

- Business cards to be made available.

- Distinctive and appropriate logo to be designed and displayed on the shop window, all promotional literature and carry bags, giving further recognition and branding to the business and symbolizing value and quality.

- Initial letter drops can be made to local residents to promote the modified product range and prices (product package).

- Advertising in the Jewish News tabloid newspaper.

- Website to promote the business and its products to the customer base and affiliate networks.

- **Place:** the existing location on a main road is excellent given that it is in the middle of a busy shopping strip that services a dense residential area, and therefore, a change in business address is not planned or required at this stage.

(ii) Sales/market share

The business will aim to have a turnover of $160,000 compared to the total projected turnover of all shops of

$1,462,480 (based on market analysis). Therefore, the business will attempt to increase its market share from 10% currently to 11%. This is a realistic objective, as the overall market is only projected to have a flat growth for the year.

4.4   KEY ASSUMPTIONS

Underpinning any set of robust business objectives is a well thought out and reasonable set of assumptions. Although the future is always a gamble, past and present trends can be used as a means of projecting future performance in conjunction with key assumptions.

If the market that your business operates in has had a consistent 2% yearly dollar growth over the last 10 years, it is unlikely it will now go much above this, unless there has been some fundamental change to the market or customers' attitudes.

Market growth rates in particular for established markets are largely stable and although sometimes subject to seasonal variation, are not generally prone to huge spikes from one year to the next. So if all other factors were held fairly constant, it would be unreasonable to assume that in the coming year the market will grow by 10%.

A 2% projected growth rate would be a reasonable assumption in this setting given the past and prevailing trends. The greater the projection above 2%, the greater the risk it will be incorrect.

For example, consider that your business currently has a 5% market share in the local market and the total local market is currently worth $10 million dollars per annum. If you believe that a market currently growing at 2% will now grow at 10%, you would project your sales to be $550,000 (i.e. 5% of $11 million) as opposed to $510,000 (i.e. 5% of $10.2 million). To begin with, this equates to a significant variance of $40,000, which the business is unlikely to earn this year. Additionally, given that this figure will be the basis for income projections for future years, it is simple to see how any unreasonable assumption today can continue to profoundly affect projections well into the future.

KEEP IN MIND

The bottom line with assumptions is to review them regularly, along with your objectives and be constantly on the lookout for any that appear to be out of kilter with what is happening in the current setting.

SUMMARY

- Business objectives must be set on an annual basis.

- Business objectives include both operational and marketing objectives.

- Operational objectives include financial, personnel and where applicable, production objectives.

- Marketing objectives include deciding on the target market, the marketing mix objectives (for product, price, promotion and place), and the market share objectives.

- All business objectives should be S.M.A.R.T i.e. Smart, Measurable, Achievable, Realistic and with Time related details.

- Key assumptions need to be made and recorded when setting objectives.

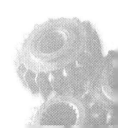

The challenge in business is about overcoming obstacles...

STAGE C:
THE MARKETING BLUEPRINT

Once you have segmented the market and decided on which particular market segment(s) to target, you are then in a position to write a marketing blueprint. The marketing blueprint will contain the interrelated  strategies for the marketing mix (i.e. the 4 Ps: product, price, promotion, and place).

From the diagram below, it can be seen how the targeted customer is the focus of the strategic development of the marketing mix. The four Ps will each be addressed in detail later in this chapter.

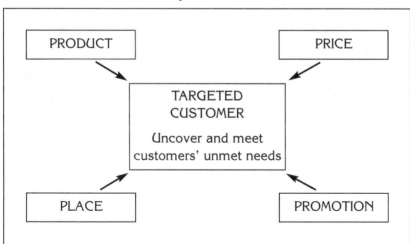

5.1 HOW TO ATTRACT CUSTOMERS TO YOUR BUSINESS: UNCOVER THE UNMET NEEDS

Quite simply, it all begins and ends with the customers' **unmet** needs. How well you are accurately able to uncover and meet these  unmet needs, will ultimately determine how successful you will be in attracting and retaining this group of targeted customers.

Unless you are talking about a new product in a new market, which currently has no existing customers, the customers you are trying to attract to your business (i.e. targeting), are already someone else's customers. Putting it another way, they are already having their needs met to some extent.

Behavioral scientists have shown repeatedly through their research, that most individuals are creatures of habit. Most people will have the same breakfast cereal each day, wear the same types of clothes, and drive the same brand of car over the years, and so on.

This is a mixed blessing for businesses. On the one hand, if you already have a customer that feels satisfied with your product offering, they will be reluctant to switch to an alternative. However, it is equally difficult to get customers to switch to your product or service from another provider.

For this type of change to occur, you must offer something over and above what is currently being offered. In other words, you must add value by fulfilling any outstanding unmet needs.

Customers may not always be conscious of the full scope of their needs, and it is not until they see something else being offered by another business, that they perceive the additional value of their offering.

KEEP IN MIND

Needs versus Unmet Needs: The unmet need is simply the gap between what is currently being offered and what is still needed which creates the opportunity for your business.

EXAMPLE: Going beyond need to unmet need

A good example of this is the story of Dial - a - Dinos. If ever you want an example of a market that is saturated with similar (mostly small) businesses with essentially the same product offering, then the pizza market is the classic illustration. The market leader, by the way at the time of this example, was and remains Pizza Hut.

Examine this case then from the perspective of customer needs. The customer's need could have been defined as requiring a delicious pizza made from fresh ingredients and available at a reasonable price that is within a reasonable distance from the customer's location. Clearly this need was met and filled by countless pizza shops.

What Dial - a - Dinos did next was the critical step. They understood that many people found it difficult to get to the shop to pick up the pizza and even those who did have transportation would find it a lot more

EXAMPLE: *continued*

convenient if they did not have to pick up the pizza themselves. They found the unmet need!

Dial - A - Dinos became the first to offer free home delivery as a value-added service. Their advertising campaigns highlighted the benefits of the additional value being offered.

Their success on the back of finding the unmet need is now well documented. They did so well, that Pizza Hut was compelled to buy them out because of the threat they posed to their dominant market position.

WORKSHOP: Finding the Unmet Need

Define your target customer market:

_____
_____

How would your key competitors define the customer needs for this group?

_____
_____

What additional customer needs remain unmet?

_____
_____

What are the consequences for the customer if these additional needs remain unmet?

_____
_____

What additional business resources will be needed to meet these unmet needs?

_____
_____

5.2   MARKETING MIX

The 4 Ps which make up the marketing mix (although all relating to different areas), are both interrelated and interdependent. They are all important and none of the four areas can ever be put together without serious thought being given to the other three Ps, and the way that each variable relates to the customers and their unmet needs.

The actual importance of each will vary somewhat between markets, however, for the most part they are relatively equal in importance and should combine to achieve a central marketing focus.

When strategies of two or more of the Ps don't complement each other, there is something seriously wrong with these strategies. Like all good members of any team, all players aim to support and strengthen each other's position, never diminishing the performance of another player.

An effective marketing blueprint should reflect synergy among the 4 Ps. For example, a car dealer selling prestige cars will have list prices in the luxury price bracket that reflect their quality. The promotional campaign will be elegant and reflect the status associated with the brand. Finally, the location of the car lot will be in an upmarket area commensurate with branding the image of the cars.

5.2.1 PRODUCT

Products or product offerings are a combination of goods and services offered to targeted customers to satisfy their unmet needs.

In the case of a retail business, which sells personal computers to the public, what "product" is the business offering? The obvious answer is computers. However, this forms only part of the answer, because as well as the actual computer, this business (as part of its overall product offering), also offers the following:

- Latest and broad range of computers.

- Related accessories e.g. software packages, peripheral equipment such as printers, visual display units, scanners.

- Special offers e.g. free printer/scanner.

- Add-on services e.g. low Internet connection costs.

- Guarantees.

- Expert sales people i.e. friendly and trained computer consultants who can assist potential buyers on the choice of a system that meets their requirements.

- Free home delivery and installation.

- After sales service e.g. free one-hour consulting time or free half-day training session.

From this simple example above, you can see that the "product offering" is much more than just computers.

Product Offerings Are a Combination of Goods and Services

In general, most product offerings are a mixture of goods and services.

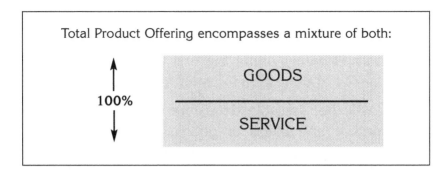

To highlight the blended nature of products, here are three simple examples.

Scenario A	Scenario B	Scenario C
100% Goods	50% Goods 50% Service	100% Service
Soft drink vending machine	Restaurant	Taxi ride

The breakdown of how much of the product is physical, versus how much is a service, varies from market to market and from business to business. However, the key point is most product offerings will be a blend of both, with only some extreme cases having only one component.

Which Products Should Your Business Sell?

Having examined what constitutes a product, the next key question is what product do you offer?

To answer this, you must take note of one key point.

CUSTOMERS BUY SATISFACTION

Customers buy **satisfaction** (not products) that comes from having their **unmet needs** met. Therefore, in determining what your product offering will look like, you must apply what you have learned earlier about the met and unmet needs of your target customers.

You will then be able determine the exact nature and blend of goods and services which contain those benefits, thereby giving SATISFACTION.

Product Management Process

By adopting a marketing approach the business is consciously following a scientific and formalized process of **product management**. Planning minimizes the role of chance. As the old adage goes, *"Businesses don't plan to fail, but do fail to plan."*

The product planning and management process (Figure 5.1) is an ongoing process of updating the product mix based on the changing needs of the targeted customers.

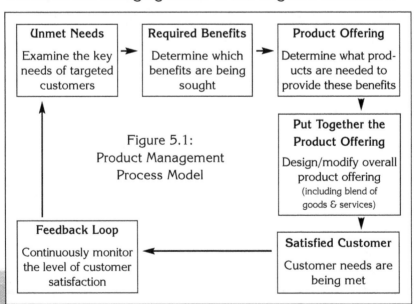

Unmet Needs

Examine the key needs of targeted customers

Required Benefits

Determine which benefits are being sought

Product Offering

Determine what products are needed to provide these benefits

Put Together the Product Offering

Design/modify overall product offering (including blend of goods & services)

Satisfied Customer

Customer needs are being met

Feedback Loop

Continuously monitor the level of customer satisfaction

Figure 5.1:
Product Management
Process Model

The process of good product management stems from understanding the needs of the customers. In having their unmet needs more fully understood, the customers derive additional satisfaction and will be more likely to continue to selectively support your product line and your business.

Branding of Products

Branding is the identification of a product by the use of any recognizable word, letter, symbol or other designation. It relates to those aspects of the product that allow it to be recognized by customers.

Some of the greatest examples of the power of branding have been connected to the birth and unparalleled growth of franchising around the world. McDonalds, Kentucky Fried Chicken, Starbucks, Subway and countless others are all examples of the strength and value of names that are virtual guarantees for success. Strong branding and recognizable brand names have a positive effect on buyer preference and loyalty.

The implications of this well accepted fact is that a business must aim to supply its market with both currently recognizable and sought after brands that have an ongoing strong consumer demand, or alternatively work to establish its own brands.

- *Why do consumers choose to buy these brands over lesser-known ones?*

Shopping is made more efficient by having major brands to choose from in each of the key product class areas. The importance of this is clear when you consider that generally there are well over 10,000 brands in the average supermarket.

Consistent quality ensures that customers' expectations are always met (sometimes even regardless of the level of quality).

Status symbols represent acceptability.

Potential for disappointment is limited by the fact that consumers (either through personal experience or referral), have a real understanding about what the product offers and the benefits it provides.

KEEP IN MIND

Consumers are in the habit of buying certain brands repeatedly and preferentially, regardless of how it performs compared to similar rival products. To change this habit, you will need to offer a product that is perceived to be significantly better at meeting the customers' needs.

- *What reasons encourage manufacturers to brand their products?*

Encourage repeat buying by effectively meeting the customers' key needs.

Develop brand loyalty through customer satisfaction.

Build a corporate image based on the perceived quality of the products being offered.

- *What are the key characteristics of a good brand name?*

Short and simple: brand names need to be memorable, as brand recognition is a key to repeat buying. Some examples of successful brand names that are short and simple include Rinso, Omo and Ford.

Easy to spell: e.g. Flora.

Easy to remember: high product recall equates to stronger brand preference e.g. Coca Cola

Pleasing to read: brand names that are pleasing to the ear are more likely to be accepted and adopted by the market e.g. Sunlight

Legally available: the business must perform a thorough search to ensure that any proposed new brand names are not already registered.

Not Offensive: ensure that any potential new brand name is not offensive in other languages or cultures.

Suggestive of product benefits: the buyer has the advantage of knowing what the product is used for e.g. Glad Wrap.

Adaptable to all advertising media: uncomplicated names will lend themselves to multimedia advertising campaigns.

Branding and Why It is So Badly Needed

Perhaps the greatest challenges facing marketers today, stems from the recent market research presented by Danish world-renowned branding expert, Martin Lindstrom. Consider the following key facts:

- By age 65, the average man has seen around 2 million TV advertisements.

- In 2004, consumer testing revealed unprompted recall of only 5% of TV advertisements tested, compared to 35% in 1965. (Ref: Source-Martin Lindstrom).

This data confirms the fact that individual products are not usually recognized by the general public or sadly, their target markets. Simply put, they do not have strong branding.

Smashing Your Brands - the Next Logical Step After Branding

Martin Lindstrom defines smashed brands as: "those that pass the test of having their logo removed from the advertisement, and yet the ad remains highly recognizable." Examples of these include: Coca Cola, McDonalds, and Absolut Vodka.

These brands have been smashed because of the consistent use of other design elements that are always present and, therefore, easily recognized and uniquely associated with the brand.

You can smash a brand in a number of ways:

- **By shape.** The definitive example of this is the shape of the Coca Cola bottle. Apart from its distinctive logo, the bottle shape is unmistakably Coke's.

- **By language.** Disney has been shown in research to own no less than six words in the English language (when it comes to advertising). They are kingdom, fantasy, dream, smile, magic and happy, with 60% of all people tested associating those words in any ad with Disney. McDonalds on the other hand has patented words with the letters "Mc" in front of them such as McShake, McNugget, etc.

- **By sound.** For this example, listen no further than the James Bond movie theme music.

- **By ritual.** There are many examples of this, but a simple one is that of using consistently misspelled words in an ad, as seen with Absolut Vodka.

Although these examples of smashed brands are from large organizations, it is important to note that huge promotional budgets do not guarantee brands to be smashed. There are many examples of large companies that had smashed a brand, but because of lack of continuing consistency in promoting that brand, have lost ownership of a recognizable symbol.

The better a brand is smashed, the greater the brand awareness. This in turn makes the brand more memorable.

Packaging

Packaging is a key part of the product offering which can make a profound difference between success and failure. Through distinctive and imaginative packaging, a business has the potential to differentiate their product from other similar products. A first rate product with inferior packaging can be unfairly dismissed in the minds of the customers because of the assumption that an inferior wrapping means an inferior product. Some recent examples of products with attractive packaging include:

- Soft Soap

- Leggs Panty Hose

- Toblerone Chocolate Bars

In general, if you have a way of packaging your product differently from your competitors then do so. This is particularly significant because many small businesses operate in highly undifferentiated markets where there is no obvious difference between the various products being offered.

This area has become so important that companies specializing in this creative packaging area are emerging. Creative packaging could, therefore, be the basis for your products to be priced, promoted and perceived differently from rival offerings in homogenous markets.

KEEP IN MIND

The right packaging is just enough packaging.

Given that only a small number of products are truly unique in the marketplace and totally differentiated from their main rivals, you need to challenge yourself and ask how you can make the packaging a little better and a little different from the others. It may be the edge that you have over your competitors.

Experiential Retailing: An Emerging Opportunity for Small Businesses to Differentiate Themselves

In recent times there has been a fundamental shift with respect to what customers expect from the shopping experience, from merely buying goods and services in the past, to now buying experiences.

Michael Morrison, Research Director of the Australian Centre for Retail Studies recently wrote:

"*The retail landscape has changed and consequently the retail shopping experience has moved through various stages, from the basic need for products and services, to a focus on leisure, fun, fantasy, entertainment, theater and now to 'experiential retailing'.*"

He went on to say that:

"*Experience has now become a key value differentiator, since consumers view price, quality and service as standard requirements. Consumers' emotions and senses are being excited by 'experiential retailing' strategies in stores like The American Girl Place, Apple, Prada and Skechers (New York City), Kenzo (Paris) and KaDeWe (Berlin) that have created retail brand difference with retail experiences that lead to competitive positioning, brand differentiation and image enhancement.*"

- *Adapt your approach to stimulate the five senses*

Retailers must proactively design their shops with the goal of positively stimulating the various senses in a way that will be pleasing to the targeted customer group.

For example, colors can be used to encourage and maintain certain moods. Lighting can also be carefully designed and positioned to further enhance the effect of the color and general ambience.

Special aromas will not only add to the overall feel of the store design, but can also be a powerful trigger to buy. Shop fittings and other materials are used to further enhance visual and tactile experiences. Finally, yet importantly, music carefully chosen can complete the total sensory experience for the customer.

> ### EXAMPLE
>
> Borders Book stores are relaxing to be in. They are purposefully designed to get people to stay for long periods.
>
> The music is soft and non-intrusive. The walls are painted in soft colors which are easy on the eye. The carpet is thick and very comfortable to walk on. Simply put, all elements in the store work together to strengthen the relaxing theme and complete the Borders experience.

- *Strategies for creating the total retail shopping experience**

     (Used with permission from work by Michael Morrison)

  ✓ Ensure that the in-store experience fits in well with the character of the retail brand.

  ✓ Design stores that are unique, special and distinctive.

  ✓ Integrate special events, themes and store layout that engage all the five senses of customers.

  ✓ Reinforce the shopping experience with a take-away/promotional item.

  ✓ Incorporate entertainment, education, aesthetics and escapism elements into the total shopping experience.

  *michael.morrison@buseco.monash.edu.au

  *Professional Marketing, July 2004, pp26-27.

Rebranding – Relaunching Existing Brands

How and when do you relaunch an existing brand back onto the market?

When you relaunch is perhaps the easier question to answer. It is likely to happen when you have a product that is not being accepted by the market. If you have an inferior product, the answer could be quite simple - you delete the product line. However, you may have a good quality product that is not performing for reasons other than quality.

Three key steps are the same for any rebranding project:

- Develop the essence of the brand (i.e. what does the brand truly stand for).

- Develop a new logo and packaging to project the image that supports that essence.

- Ensure that all language and promotional communication is congruent with the new image and brand essence.

EXAMPLE: Rebranding an Existing Quality Product

Years ago, Black and Decker had a high quality power drill that had only modest sales and low market share despite it being technically as good as or better than the market leader. At the time, the product was being targeted to professional tradesmen who needed industrial strength power tools.

The irony of this story is that this particular brand although first rate in terms of quality looked very similar in shape and color to a domestic power tool used by

EXAMPLE: *continued*

non-professionals. Not surprisingly, the target market, who wanted their tools to look and perform better than those used by lay people, rejected the brand.

Once the makers realized why the brand had failed to fulfil the unmet need of the target market, they rebranded the same product and relaunched it in a striking new color, with a new brand name and distinctive logo that reflected the characteristics of what the tradesmen wanted in their power tools. With the unmet need now met, this relaunched brand went on to be highly successful and profitable for its maker.

This is a simple example of how a business can rebrand a struggling product and eventually build up that relaunched brand to a point where eventually it can be smashed.

EXAMPLE: Rebranding on a Far Bigger Scale

More recently, a far bigger rebranding occurred when BHP Steel was relaunched as Blue Scope Steel.

Blue Scope Steel Corporate Brand Manager, Leo Kerema was charged with the responsibility of overseeing the rebranding of BHP Steel to its new corporate form, Blue Scope Steel. Using the core values of the BHP Steel brand, aspects of the new brand, including the new name, logo, promotional materials were created.

Such has been the success of this relaunch that a review in the Financial Review (Sunday Sun - Oct 31, 2004) noted:

> **EXAMPLE:** *continued*
>
> *"..... excellent strategy executed with military precision and timing.....with the share price rising from $2.85 to $8.80."*

Clearly, rebranding can be done either with individual product brands or entire companies. If you feel you need to rebrand some aspect of your business, there is a simple model that may help (see Figure 5.2).

To identify the true essence and core value of your brand, you need to work through each stage of the pyramid beginning at the bottom.

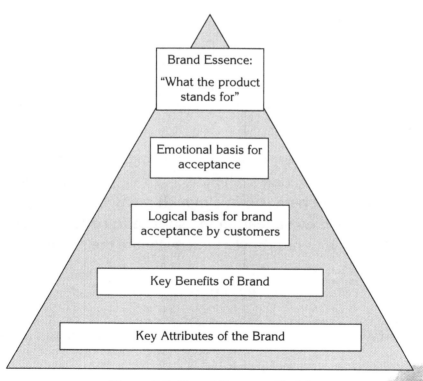

Figure 5.2: Brand Essence Model

Value Services: Yet Another Area Where Small Businesses Can be Larger

Small businesses have greater potential for providing better value-added services to their target customers compared to their bigger competitors. Whereas big business operates across vast geographical areas and produce identical goods and services for all customers in each branch and in each state, in line with the overall corporate strategy, small business has the advantage of being able to modify and customize their services for any given customer need.

This flexibility is a distinct advantage small businesses have, allowing a more personal bond with the customers, thereby adding to the level of customer satisfaction and loyalty.

In a market where the product offering is homogenous and the customers perceive no clear-cut differences among the competing products, services perceived to be of better value could differentiate your business from the rest.

These services could be anything from improved telephone answering techniques to free home delivery. The key point here is that although many of these types of services may appear on the surface to be fairly basic in nature, you must never underestimate their value.

KEEP IN MIND

Think about which existing services could be improved or introduced to more exactly meet your customers' needs.

EXAMPLE

A young couple in Queensland Australia rents out their two holiday apartments in an area where there are literally thousands of apartments within a few minutes drive of each other.

Understandably, the young couple does not want to merely compete on price, as a price war will eventuate and their product will still remain undifferentiated in the longer term. Understanding this situation, they proceed to introduce services that others do not.

They routinely meet their new tenants on their arrival and whenever possible, pick the tenants up from the airport to make the process less taxing for them. Additionally, the owners are there on departure to ensure that the tenants' stay has been a pleasant one. Once in the apartment, the tenants will find a welcome gift which helps ensure a positive first impression. Moreover, they are given a parting gift as a reminder of their stay.

Using this approach the couple have had a high occupancy rate of over 80% for both apartments, which is well above the rate experienced historically by the area in general. This example highlights how small businesses have the power to go the extra mile and compete in even the most competitive of established markets.

5.2.2 PROMOTION: REVENUE GENERATORS

As previously discussed, each business operates with the expressed purpose of solving a particular set of need related problems for a given group of customers.

Promotion is the process by which the business can communicate with its customers and inform them on **how** it will meet their needs.

This section will deal with all areas of promotion for small businesses, detailing the various options, pros and cons, and relative costs of each.

It is, however, prudent at this stage to dispel the notion held by many small businesses, that promotion is not necessary when running a small business.

Many people involved in small business argue they have survived many years with varying degrees of success by referrals alone. Others add they are very successful with minimal amount of promotion, thereby minimizing costs. Simply put, they believe that, "If you build a better mouse trap, the world will beat a path to your door."

The reality is that a business that is "surviving" could potentially be prospering and those that are thriving could be doing even better still. In this day of intense competition, it is no longer enough to provide the exact product, to a specific target market. The better "mousetrap" is still required, but should be coupled with an aggressive and well-planned promotion to ensure that targeted customers are made fully aware of what you have to offer and more importantly, what they have to gain.

Often small businesses are run on comparatively small operating budgets and, therefore, funds for promotion may appear difficult to justify. However, a relatively small amount spent on the correct promotional blend in the longer term makes money for your business. Also, remember that all promotional funds for the business are tax deductible. This is a practical, yet often forgotten, fact in business.

KEEP IN MIND

Promotion is an income generator.

Promotional Objectives

There are three main promotional objectives a business may pursue. They are to:

1. **Inform:** Example - Original Hoechst television ads (now merged into Aventis), to inform market about the company's existence, vision and broad product range.

2. **Persuade:** Example - Original Macintosh Computer television ads, specifically targeting the business sector, on the superiority of Apple Mac computers for business use.

3. **Remind:** Example - Coca-Cola ads remind the world the Coke brand is still here and going strong.

The objectives you choose for your business or brands should reflect the stage of the **product lifecycle** they are in. A couple of simple questions will need to be answered to formulate the business promotional strategies.

- *To whom do you promote the business/product?*

This question could easily be rewritten as "To whom do you wish to communicate with?" The answer is, all promotional activities should be directed to and formulated with the target customers in mind.

It is well known that funds spent on promotional activities (e.g. sales promotions, advertising, etc), can often be poorly applied and subsequently wasted.

Lord Leverhulme (of Lever & Kitchen) actually went as far as to say that, "50% of money spent on advertising is wasted, but which 50%?"

Wastefulness occurs when a business loses sight of its primary promotional objective, which is to attract people from specifically selected market segments.

Large businesses given their huge resources are often guilty of being a little wasteful with advertising, but small businesses (that do not have millions in their promotional budget) must aim to be precise. A business requires more than just demographics, such as age and income to understand its target market. It needs to focus on its needs, attitudes, beliefs, usage patterns, etc.

As mentioned earlier, you should try to write a half to one-page profile regarding your targeted customer. This will help you visualize each potential customer as a single individual rather than as part of a group. It is a useful tool for answering this first question as well as the remaining questions.

- *What does the business want to communicate in its promotions?*

The communication should include how the business and its product offering(s) will fulfill the unmet needs of the customers. It is as simple *and* as complex as that.

To do this you will need to:

1. Go to the essence of the product.

2. Ask: "What does the product do for the customer?"

3. Develop a key proposition, which is a simple statement that embodies the core message of exactly what makes your product special. For example, in the Apple Macintosh example above, the key proposition is potent and simple: Business Superiority.

The business has targeted a specific group of customers and plans to offer a particular product offering to satisfy a particular need. Therefore, the content of your promotion (be it public relations, advertising etc.) should communicate the product benefits that will fulfill that particular need.

Remember, customers do not buy products. They buy satisfaction from product benefits. Therefore, good promotional activity will always aim to spell out in simple terms how this will be accomplished.

Promotional Alternatives Available to the Business

The four main promotional options available to your business are advertising, public relations, personal selling and sales promotion.

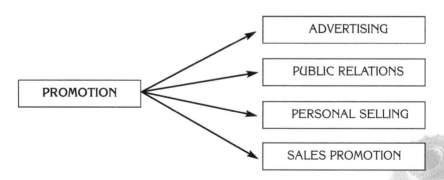

Advertising

Advertising is a paid form of non-personal presentation of products (comprising goods and/or services).

KEEP IN MIND

Advertising is what you do if you can't go and see someone.

The business must determine what it wishes to achieve in advertising. These **advertising objectives** should complement the overall marketing effort.

It is essential that all advertising objectives are written in such a way that they are specific and, therefore, measurable. This is an example of an inadequate advertising objective: "The advertising campaign aims to increase the number of people who come through the store."

It is not known how many more people are expected to come into the store over a given period of time. A better advertising objective may be: "The advertising campaign will increase the number of people visiting the shop by 20% inside of 2 months", **or** "The advertising campaign will increase the number of telephone inquiries by 10% inside of 1 month."

The advertising objectives will influence the kind of advertising required. There are two main types of advertising. They are product advertising and institutional advertising.

Product Advertising – aims to sell a particular good and/or service by increasing customer awareness, interest and demand for that product offering. There are four sub-sets of this form of advertising. They are:

a. **Pioneering Advertising** – attempts to create demand for an overall product type rather than a specific brand of product. It is used to build aware-ness and inform potential customers about new products on the market. An example of pioneering advertising would be advertising to promote DVD players, where initially the object was not to pro-mote a particular brand, but the new concept of the DVD player itself i.e. to build **primary demand**.

b. **Competitive Advertising** – unlike pioneering advertising which aims to build primary demand, competitive advertising attempts to build demand for a specific product brand. This is called sec-ondary demand. Relating this to the earlier exam-ple of the DVD player, it can be seen that as the general public gradually became more aware and informed about DVD technology, advertising then attempted to push specific brands and models to its target markets.

c. **Comparative Advertising** – when a particular brand of product is regarded as superior, a specific form of competitive advertising called comparative adver-tising can be deployed to place the advertised prod-uct head-to-head with the competitor. An example of this is the "Energizer" television commercial which describes how "Energizer" lasts longer than "Duracell." This is a powerful form of advertising which can build strong, selective demand if a prod-uct is perceived to be superior to its opposition. Overall, competitive advertising is used after the general public has become reasonably familiar with the product.

d. **Reminder Advertising** – is used for well estab-lished brands. The classic example of this form of advertising is Coca-Cola advertising. This is a product which is the market leader (world-wide) and yet, its makers understand the need for con-tinual reminder advertising to keep the product constantly in the minds of its target audience.

Institutional Advertising – aims to influence and shape people's perceptions and attitudes regarding the business itself. By doing this it attempts to improve goodwill, market posture and general public opinion among customers, sup-pliers, distributors and even employees. Examples of this type of advertising include those for BHP and Bluescope. As with comparative advertising, institutional advertising is usually undertaken by large organizations such as the above, McDonalds and the Bank of America.

There are a variety of advertising media i.e. electronic and passive. Selecting the most appropriate type of media is easy once a clear set of advertising objectives are set.

Electronic media includes television, radio and the Internet, whereas passive (non-electronic) media includes newspapers, magazines, outdoor advertising and direct mail. This section of the book will address the advantages and disadvantages of each of these advertising tools.

Television

Advantages:

- Television sells everything (products, corporations, serials etc).

- Great impact.

- Complete total medium (sound, color, emotion, shock).

- Mass coverage (almost everyone has access to a television today).

- Repetition leads to a lasting impression.

- Flexibility.

- Prestige.

- Low cost per contact made.

Disadvantages:

- Temporary message as the ad is only on for a few seconds each time it is on.

- Highest overall cost of all media, both for production of ad and airtime.

- Ads usually have a short life span.

- Lack of selectivity, as it is often difficult to target specific audiences with any certainty.

Costs:

- Variable depending on time of advertising and cost of producing advertisements. A thirty second ad will cost around $5,000 - $10,000 in airtime.

Overview:

Television is the media with the greatest reach at a low cost per contact made, however it is still expensive overall. It is used to develop long term branding campaigns. Although not traditionally the medium of small business, the advent of direct marketing campaigns have made this form of media more viable to small business and a real option to gain widespread exposure.

Radio

Advantages:

- Usually easy to access.
- Intimacy with listening audience.
- Low cost (good for low budget).
- Indepth market research potentially available to make it easier to accurately target audience.
- Mobility (walkmans, car stereo, etc).

Disadvantages:

- Fragmentation of audience does not always lend itself to products that have mass appeal.
- Transience of message.
- Market research information is potentially not available on audience demographics, especially in smallers markets.
- No visual component.

Costs:

- $500 - $1,000 per 30 seconds, plus the cost of producing the ad.

Overview:

It has been said that radio is the theater of the mind. It can stretch the imagination and remains the most personal form of media, where the listener feels the announcer is speaking on a one-to-one basis, therefore, forming a strong bond. Due to inexpensive costs, radio advertising can be structured for reach and frequency. Your costs include both the airtime and the cost of producing the ad.

Internet

Advantages:

- Potential access to virtually every global customer with Internet access.

- Most cost effective form of promotion in terms of cost per contact.

- Lends itself to effectively promoting any type of product.

- Relatively inexpensive to set up website and /or email campaigns.

Disadvantages:

- Low conversion rates i.e. only about 1% of people who see the ad will buy the product.

- Only 1 in 20 Internet users currently buy anything on the Internet.

- Mailing lists are often inaccurate and become quickly outdated.

- Advertising by email can be perceived as invasive by some customers.

Costs:

- Website design can vary from a few thousand to $20,000 depending on size and function.

- Maintenance costs vary from approximately $30/month to hundreds.

- Mailing lists for email campaigns range from 5 cents to 20 cents per contact.

- Merchant banking costs – refer to your preferred bank for specifics.

Overview:

Without a doubt, the Internet has become the most powerful and revolutionary form of promotion available to any business, large or small. Businesses are increasingly able to more accurately target specific customer groups by email and promote their full range of products in a cost effective way.

Earlier this year, President of Nielsen//Netratings in Asia Pacific / Latin America, Richard Webb, presented new research data, which spells out exactly why advertising on the Internet is no longer just an optional form of promotion.

Currently 14% of all advertising is done through the Internet. It is the fastest growing form of promotion accounting for about 4.8% of all promotional spending.

Furthermore, it is now the preferred option for most customer research. Consumers are now spending $1 on the net for every $1.70 they spend offline. In Australia alone with a population of 20 million, over 11 million people were online by the beginning of 2006.

Perhaps the most incredible statistic presented by the former Red Sheriff chief is that with all this presence, growth and expansion of the Internet, to date only 3% of all commerce is transacted on the net. Imagine the remaining potential!

Early horror stories of credit card abuse have had a profound dampening effect on people's acceptance of the Internet as a safe mode of buying, but as security systems become increasingly sophisticated, the vast majority will no doubt soon discover the advantages of shopping online.

Sensis Search Group Manager, Dr. Elisabet Wreme believes that the future of the Internet will have two key emergent trends:

- Functionality of the net will continue to improve with more advanced technology making ecommerce more efficient and safer.

- Channels will further segment the population using the Internet, which will allow businesses to more accurately separate their targeted customers from the rest of the market.

Businesses need to embrace the net by gradually increasing their advertising spent there and plan how they can gain the required knowledge and skills to compete effectively with other e-equipped rivals. As Dr. Wreme stated:

"The Internet is the new component in the arsenal of available tools to get your products into the market. It won't replace other advertising, just augment it."

Based on the prevailing global trends and the unstoppable march of broadband into homes and businesses, it becomes clear that Internet advertising is the future and those businesses that can quickly adapt, will no doubt be the ones to benefit most.

Newspapers

Advantages:

- Flexibility (Bookings Monday for Friday).

- Community Prestige.

- Intense Coverage.

- Reader control of exposure i.e if the reader is interested, he/she can take extra time.

- Coordination of advertising (national) campaign is fairly simple.

Disadvantages:

- Short life span (1 to 7 days approximately).

- Reading is usually hasty.

- Poor reproduction quality, especially compared to magazines.

Cost:

- Advertising cost per page: major city paper - approximately $5,000 for a quarter page; local papers - approximately $1,000 - $2,000 per quarter page.

Overview:

Newspapers are easy to advertise in and widely read, but the problem is that the advertising generally has limited 'stopping' ability, therefore, it may not always succeed in getting people's attention. In short, it needs a strong visual "hook."

Magazines

Advantages:

- Selectivity to focus on precise trade/market.
- Quality reproduction.
- Long life.
- Prestige associated with a good publication.
- Fairly detailed messages possible.

Disadvantages:

- Fairly inflexible due to long lead times.

Cost:

- Relatively expensive per page ($10,000 - $20,000 per page).

Overview:

Magazines are useful for longer term branding and positioning of a business and its products. They can help establish awareness and inform people with fairly detailed messages.

Outdoor Advertising

Advantages:

- Repetition.
- Localized exposure.
- Quality graphics available.

- Fairly inexpensive per contact.

Disadvantages:

- Brief message.
- Public concern over aesthetics.
- Not possible to segment audience.

Cost:

- Variable expense depending on location and time of duration of advertisement. Can range from $5,000 to $20,000.

Overview:

Outdoor advertising, such as billboards, can be useful in delivering simple messages in the form of reminder advertising, for products and businesses which are already fairly well established and, therefore, have a reasonable amount of branding and recognizability. It is not ideal for new products which are not recognizable. The objective is a strong visual image with shopping power to attract the attention of passers-by.

Direct Mail

Advantages:

- Selectivity of mailing list.
- Intense coverage available.
- Flexibility in letter format.
- Complete information can be included.
- Can be personalized to each member of target list.
- Speed.

- Relatively cheap for a simple mailer.

Disadvantages:

- High cost per contact ($1.00 - $50.00)

- Some customer lists are not always available or may have many inaccuracies in them.

- Consumer resistance based on widespread attitude that the promotional material is mostly unsolicited.

- Potentially slow response time.

- Often low response rates at 1% or less.

Cost:

- Cost depends on how many letters or mailers are produced and sent.

- Greatest cost is often the production cost, which is independent of the number of letters produced. Depending on print quality, production cost can be as high as $10,000-$20,000 per campaign.

- Printing and mailing costs are directly related to the size of the mailing list.

Overview:

These days, fairly reliable and extensive mailing lists are generally available and accurate so that a business can advertise to a specific target market. Mail drops can be delivered relatively cheaply and quickly from house to house in a given area. Generally, a viable option for local services such as gardening, carpet cleaning, etc.

- *What is the best media for you?*

There is no definitive answer to this question. Each business must determine how appropriate each alternative is in relation to:

1. Its target market.

2. The budget available to the business for advertising.

3. Its advertising objectives .

4. The promotional objectives (persuade, inform or remind).

For example, a small supermarket is more likely to make good use of newspaper advertisements, where it can focus on different products it wishes to highlight or discount, instead of elaborate glossy magazine advertisements.

On the other hand, a women's clothing store that has the next season's stock based on fashion trends abroad, would optimize the coverage available through glossy magazines and possibly back the advertisement through some electronic media.

The type of electronic media would again depend on their advertising objectives. Whether to advertise on radio or television, could partially depend on how large the advertising budget is.

Remember, you must always relate your choice of media back to your target market. Will your customers or potential customers be seeing your ads? Clearly certain media options are essential for certain types of markets. Some examples of these include advertisements for industrial markets in trade journals and advertisements for pharmaceutical products in medical journals.

Any remaining funds spent on other media will strengthen the awareness and interest stimulated by your main media choice.

There is no magic formula to media selection.

- *Developing "Good Copy"*

Having now decided on which type of advertising and which advertising media you will adopt, the business has effectively answered **"how"** it will communicate with its targeted customers using its advertising options.

The next step is to make a decision regarding **"what"** will be said in the advertisement i.e. what your **"copy"** will say, whether it is oral, written, a moving picture or illustrated form.

Good copy depends on giving the right message. The right message will vary from product to product, but the formula remains the same:

1. Go to the essence of the product (Build in the benefits).

2. What does it do for the customer (How are their needs met)?

3. Develop key proposition (Statement that embodies what the customer wants).

Examples include:

- suntan lotion: "Lasts four times longer in water."

- laundry detergent: "Washes your clothes whiter."

By adhering to these three basic points, any business can be confident of producing copy that will be appropriate for its selected target market and be precise in the communication of key propositions.

- *Who handles the advertising?*

Although a small business has the option of going to a specialist advertising agency, the relatively high costs associated with this option generally makes it impractical to do so.

It is, however, possible to organize your own advertising without going to a specialist agency group. If you have a sound understanding of the key advertising message, you can simply approach the various media options and discuss your needs with their respective media representatives.

- *A final note on advertising*

An excellent advertisement (regardless of type or media) should consistently meet three criteria:

1. **Stopping Power:** Also referred to as a "hook" i.e. how it can stop a customer and get him/her to take notice.

2. **Relevance:** Once the ad catches the customer's attention, the advertising must be relevant to the product. If not, the reader or listener may feel betrayed.

3. **Branding:** All advertisements must echo characteristics of the distinguishing brand.

In advertising, your 'signature' is very important eg. "the glass and a half of milk" is an unmistakable branding for Cadbury chocolate.

KEEP IN MIND

Branding is not the size of the logo; it is everything you do consistently.

Public Relations

Public relations (or publicity), unlike advertising, is a form of promotion where the business can potentially have little control over what is said.

Publicity usually appears in editorial, lifestyle or new-product sections of print media and/or on consumer watch segments on television and radio shows. In such situations, the publicity can cost nothing to the business. The downside to this is that the review might not be positive.

It should be noted that although the actual publicity is 'free', larger companies do pay public relations firms to facilitate good publicity about their products and image.

More important than the cost of publicity, is the fact that publicity carries with it a reliance on objective, editorial perspective which the general public accepts and trusts. Therefore, publicity carries more credibility than conventional advertising

Quite literally, "the proof of the pudding is in the eating." The best example of this is a restaurant review. If you read a complimentary review of a newly opened restaurant in the lifestyle section of a newspaper, you are more likely to believe this than if the same restaurant advertised on television or radio.

To obtain good publicity, your product or business must be newsworthy (in a positive sense).

KEEP IN MIND

Publicity when properly utilized can be a powerful tool in successfully promoting the business and its products to the target market.

Despite this potential, however, it remains the least used and most underdeveloped form of promotion, by small businesses in particular.

Personal Selling

The third form of promotion available to business is personal selling. As the phrase suggests, this method involves face-to-face contact between a representative of the business (eg. a store salesperson, on-road sales representative, or other member of the sales force) and a current or potential customer.

This type of promotion has some unique qualities and when applicable, is an indispensable part of the business promotional package.

Advantages:

1. Flexibility

The salesperson can tailor or vary the standard sales presentation and message in creative ways to more closely meet the different needs of individual customers. In this way the business can incorporate flexibility in its dealings with customers which is not found in any other form of promotion. This flexibility can take many forms. For example, the business can establish price parameters (i.e. maximum and minumum prices) for a given product and the salesperson can vary the final price based on various factors.

2. Two-way communication

Unlike the one-way communication found in the other promotional options, communication in personal selling is two-way and importantly, it can be extended in terms of the time taken to more precisely convey what needs to be said and answer any questions that arise.

3. Ability to close a sale

Another unique feature of personal selling is that the salesperson is in a position to actually take an order, thereby, finalizing details and closing the sale. No matter how good your advertising, public relations or sales promotions are, they never close a sale.

4. Provision of market feedback

Sales people are the best source of feedback to obtain accurate and timely information regarding customers' views and needs. This ongoing source of information on all aspects of the current promotion will not only enhance awareness of the current situation in the market place, but will also help to refine the business strategy and message into the future.

Disadvantage:

The main disadvantage is low exposure i.e. fewer people are exposed to the promotion within a finite time, when compared to electronic media where millions of people can be exposed to a company's product by viewing, hearing or reading a single advertisement.

* *How many sales people are needed?*

The actual number and function of a business sales force will, of course, vary from one business to the other. A well trained sales force and the essential role they play, however, cannot be underestimated or substituted in any other way.

Only when a business can be certain that its sales force is large enough to satisfy customer demands, will it be large enough. Any smaller and your customers' needs will not be met.

A salesforce can be broken down into various kinds of salespeople who perform different functions. Briefly, these have been divided in the following way:

Retail store sales people:

People who serve over the counter in a traditional retail interface between the business and it's customers. These positions are often referred to as sales assistants or sales clerks. Their function is to see to the needs of any person who enters the store looking to purchase a particular product.

Representatives:

Representatives refer to those salespeople who go to the target market on behalf of the company to promote the product and drive sales.

Field Supervisors:

They are usually more technically oriented and complement the efforts of the other sales people when more specific, scientific or technical knowledge is required or requested. In short, they complement the bulk of the sales force and become involved when more complex matters arise that may be beyond the scope of a representative's know-how.

- *What constitutes a good salesperson?*

Regardless of what type of salespeople are employed, there are some basic elements which are common to all good salespeople.

1. Good salespeople first listen to the customer— they listen for unmet needs, objections, fears and uncertainties.

2. Good salespeople have empathy with their customers—this is sensed by customers and helps develop a solid business relationship.

3. Good salespeople are problem solvers—they manipulate various elements of the marketing mix, thereby, making the product offering more attractive to the customer.

4. Good salespeople are persuasive, but NOT pushy—there is a fine line between an assertive salesperson who works to achieve a mutual goal and an aggressive salesperson who aims to achieve only selfish goals. The first is essential and the other is intolerable.

5. Good salespeople progress the call. Years ago, it was demanded of sales people to close every

call with a sale. In these more enlightened times, it has been realized that this is not realistic as the customer may not be ready to buy at that stage. Even so, this does not mean that the representative cannot bring the customer a little closer to buying the product.

- *Motivation determines performance*

Different salespeople have varying levels of self-motivation. A business must also do its part to contribute to high levels of motivation by establishing an environment which recognizes and consistently rewards good performance. This can be done through increases in salaries or bonuses if sales targets are met or exceeded.

By setting up this win-win structure, the salesforce can have a share in the success of the business.

- *A closer look at what the business must do to keep it's employees motivated*

It is safe to say that for sales representatives to be able to operate at consistently high levels of motivation, they must above all else, feel inspired. A **culture** that will facilitate and sustain this has to be created.

Kevin Panozza, the Managing Director of Salesforce Australia, defines culture as: "The sum of all the enthusiasm, imagination and dynamic energy of all the people who are at the business."

What does a business need to consistently do to keep its people inspired and motivated?

As winners of The 2004 Hewitt Award for Best Australian Employer, Salesforce Australia have adopted the following 3 F motivational model to attain this culture:

Key Element	Key Functional Aspects of Element
Fun	Those activities, systems and processes that help to engender a sense of fun in all aspects of work life.
Focus	Key focus on encouragement, training and moral support that the employee receives on an ongoing basis.
Fulfillment	System of praise, awards, incentives and recognition designed to reward and recognize employees based on their accomplishments.

(3)F Motivational Model – Adapted from Salesforce Australia.

The ongoing passion and level of motivation of individual salespeople can inspire and energize customers. As well as this direct effect, there is another less obvious benefit that comes from having an inspired salesforce who build strong relationships and meet customer needs. This benefit is 'word-of-mouth.' Research has consistently shown that this type of unpaid publicity carries with it the highest levels of credibility and power to positively influence, given that the referrals usually come from a colleague or friend.

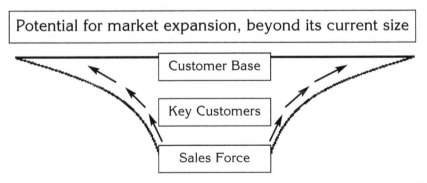

Potential for market expansion, beyond its current size

Customer Base

Key Customers

Sales Force

Figure 5.3: Influential Relationship Model

KEEP IN MIND

Whether or not you have a motivated, well-trained sales person
can mean the difference between
success and failure.

Sales Promotion

Sales promotion is the name given to those special promotions the business offers consumers, trade and sales forces, outside of advertising, publicity, personal selling and normal pricing.

Its function or purpose is to stimulate trial, interest and eventual purchase of the product by customers. Examples include: contests, give-aways, more product for the same price, etc.

The 1920s and 1930s marked the advent of 'sales promotion' in the USA, when manufacturing companies (already using advertising and the other promotional methods) wanted another tool to increase their market share and net profits. Interestingly, the term 'sales promotion' was not coined until the 1950s.

Sales promotion can be seen as a short term activity with a limited run. The business adopts these sales promotion activities in between periods of advertising.

- *Key targets for sales promotion*
  1. The Customers
  2. The Trade (eg. wholesalers, retailers, manu-facturers, etc.)

3. The Sales Force

There are many examples of sales promotion for each of these three target groups:

To The Customer:

- Introductory offer on 20% more laundry detergent in each box for one month (premium).

- Send three labels back and receive money (rebate).

- Buy a set of golf clubs and enter competition for two tickets to this year's British Open (contest).

- Free samples of product e.g. shampoo delivered to household mailboxes or given away with purchases over $10.00 at retail outlet (sampling).

To the Trade:

- A manufacturer offers retailers 10% discount on a new product during a two month introductory period.

- Retailers offer a manufacturer two months of free local advertising.

- Manufacturer produces visually impressive point of purchase material to attract customers.

To the Salesforce:

- Business offers an end of year trip to the salesperson who sells the most products.

- Cash bonuses for achieving and exceeding predetermined personal sales objectives.

- Manufacturer offers a free gift/cash incentive to salesforce or any salesperson who can sell 100 units of a product into any given store in one week.

- Training courses to sales staff in areas of interest as a reward for outstanding sales.

KEEP IN MIND

Sales Promotion works in short, sharp bursts.

Overview:

Sales promotion, like public relations, is an under developed promotional tool. When used properly, it can be an effective device in increasing sales by stimulating interest, trial and eventual repeat purchasing.

Rather than taking the place of the more major forms of promotion like advertising and personal selling, sales promotion should be a complement. Overall, it remains a strong promotional option for small business today, as the costs of performing these sales promotion activities are usually offset by the increase in demand.

The most successful sales promotions are the ones that are original. Be creative and come up with something a little different.

SUMMARY

The four main promotional options available to your business are advertising, public relations, personal selling and sales promotion.

Promotion is ongoing; therefore, try to spread your promotional effort throughout the year. Some periods

> **SUMMARY** *continued*
>
> will require more promotion funds than others, but regular promotion will sustain the customer awareness of the business and its products. Vary the form of promotion based on the promotional objectives.
>
> All promotional activities should be developed with the targeted customer in mind. Always ask whether the target market is likely to understand, appreciate, and respond positively to proposed promotions.

5.2.3 PRICE

The golden rule of pricing is well known, but often forgotten. The price of any product should reflect not just what you want, but also the value that your customers place on the product.

> **KEEP IN MIND**
>
> Something is only ever worth what your target customer is willing and able to pay for it.

Understandably, pricing strategies have always been a key area of business planning and this has never been truer than today, given the ever increasing competitive nature of pricing in virtually all markets.

Accordingly, each business must develop an understanding for setting the 'right' price for a given product at a given time and place. This section will now examine all areas of pricing and discuss how a business determines which price is the right price.

Pricing Strategies

There are three broad pricing strategies the business can adopt to determine the pricing of any one product or group of products. It is important to understand that the same product would be priced differently in the same target market, with a different pricing strategy.

1. Profit oriented pricing strategy

This strategy takes the view that profits should be maximized at the expense of market share by setting as high a product selling price as the market will accept.

This is the traditional pricing strategy when the aim is to gain optimum short-term profit. Here the business formulates its selling price by adding the cost of the product and that of the desired mark up (to cover additional costs and trade margin). This method calculates price from the business perspective and in no real way considers the level of consumer demand generated at different price levels.

Profit oriented (or skimming) pricing policy is an effective strategy only under certain circumstances:

- When the business has a **monopoly** in a given market or segment of market e.g. where the product is unique.

- In relation to luxury goods, where the highest price is perceived as higher quality in certain markets and actually stimulates increased sales.

Given that most businesses do not deal in monopoly market situations or luxury markets, skimming pricing policies are not generally appropriate.

2. Sales oriented pricing strategy

Sales oriented pricing strategies are adopted by businesses that wish to maximize their unit sales. This is done by implementing a penetration pricing policy, where the business attempts to sell its product to its target market at a price that is as low as possible, with the aim of securing as much market share as possible.

This method of pricing is generally very effective in most markets that are very competitive and price sensitive. Here there is little differentiation between the product offerings from competing businesses and as a result, the one with the most competitive price becomes the most attractive to customers at a given time. This method is most appropriate for inexpensive, high volume products.

In many cases, this policy is used for a limited time to gain market share and acceptance by the market. When the business position strengthens in a given market, the prices can be gradually increased in search of increased profit.

3. Market/status quo pricing strategy

This strategy is used by businesses that operate in homogeneous (undifferentiated) markets. Pricing competition is avoided as it stimulates price wars with subsequent decreases in profit.

This strategy is very common for many small businesses. Businesses that are operating in highly competitive markets prefer to compete on a non-price competition basis i.e. on the basis of the other three Ps.

Which Pricing Policy?

Most small businesses operate within 'pure competition' i.e. in homogeneous markets with low market entry barriers where both buyers and sellers have a sound knowledge of the products offered.

The acid test to determine if a market involves 'pure competition' is to see if any one business can control the price level in the market. In a legitimate 'pure competition' environment, no business (regardless of size) can do this.

This is because the demand for the particular product is **elastic**. In other words, the demand is highly responsive to changes in price and as a result, if a particular business increases their prices, their customers will buy the same product elsewhere.

In such situations there is a real danger of constant price wars between rival businesses, competing for the same part of the market. To illustrate this point, consider two menswear stores in close proximity to each other in a shopping center. It is in the interest of both to adopt a market/status quo pricing strategy and avoid any head-on competition. Instead, they should try to compete on a non-pricing basis e.g. by offering different brands of clothes, different styles, and so on.

Figure 5.4 illustrates a typical market demand and supply curve. Points A, B and C relate to the three different pricing strategies

Point A: $4.00/unit (per profit oriented pricing policy).

Point B: $3.00/unit (per market/status quo pricing policy).

Point C: $2.00/unit (per sales oriented pricing policy).

At Point A, 2,000 units would be sold at $4.00/unit; trade revenue = $8,000.

At Point B, 3,000 units would be sold at $3.00/unit; trade revenue = $9,000.

At Point C, 4,000 units would be sold at $2.00/unit; trade revenue = $8,000.

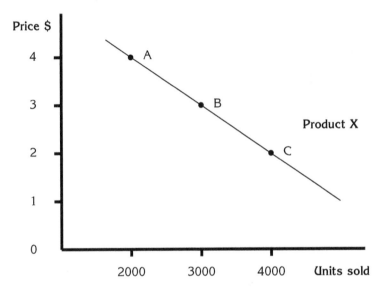

Fig 5.4: Product Demand Curve for Product X

This example shows that in a 'pure competition', homogeneous market, adopting the market/status quo pricing policy is the most effective long-term strategy. Occasional use of the sales oriented pricing policy is justified when unit sales have to be maximized.

SUMMARY

Generally speaking, small businesses are not in a position to pursue profit oriented pricing strategies, as

SUMMARY *continued*

they rarely have unique products where skimming prices can be adopted successfully.

Small businesses generally do not adopt penetration pricing under a sales oriented pricing strategy on an ongoing basis, although it can be successfully implemented on occasions when unit sales have to be maximized

Not surprisingly, small businesses are often best suited to market/status quo pricing strategies, where the other three Ps becomes the major areas of product differentiation.

5.2.4 PLACE

The fourth and final element of the marketing mix is 'place.' Place relates to getting a product to its targeted customers at the right place, time and in the right quantities and in a form that is acceptable to your customers. In other words, the "place" element refers to the distribution channel along which your product travels to reach your customers.

A typical example of the distribution channel for a business (e.g. a manufacturer) is as follows:

Manufacturer → Wholesaler → Retailer → Customer

No matter how good your product is or how well it is promoted or how reasonably it is priced, it all amounts to nothing if your customers cannot get it consistently at a convenient time and place.

KEEP IN MIND

"Place" is how and where the customers get what they need

The actual set up of the distribution channel will, of course, vary depending on the function of the business (e.g. wholesaler, retailer, etc.) and the nature of the market. Regardless, you will need to ensure that the dynamics of the distribution channel are optimal.

All decision making and details relating to distribution of your product(s) should be formalized as part of your written marketing plan. By putting on paper a current or proposed channel of distribution, the business can identify any errors or possible oversights and then progress to a superior distribution channel.

Suffice to say, many small retail businesses will have the following channel:

The location is, therefore, very important to ensure the correct target market is reached.

As the saying goes: LOCATION, LOCATION, LOCATION!

- *Transportation of stock: How does the product move?*

Consider the following:

How do your products move from your business to other members of the distribution channel? What type of transportation is required? In relation to the vehicles for transportation, do you buy or lease or do a combination of both? What are the product delivery times?

- *Inventory Level: How much of each type of product is required, when, where and how?*
    - Key decisions need to be made regarding how much of each type of product is required at various times throughout the year. There are significant consequences that stem from having either too much or too little stock.
    - Too much stock leads to product spoilage, space taken up by non-moving inventory, increased storage costs and insurance premiums. Whereas too little stock, leads to loss of faith by customers.
    - Capacity and capability to reorder quickly and efficiently from suppliers during times of unusual levels of increased demand, is a key need for the business.

- *Storage: Is it required, where and how?*

    You will need to determine the best place(s) where your product is to be stored before it is moved along your designated distribution channel. There are cost considerations to anticipate here.

SUMMARY

- The marketing blueprint outlines the interrelated marketing mix strategies, and explains how they work together to meet the needs of the target market.

- The key to attracting and holding onto customers is to go beyond the basic needs to the unmet needs and then effectively fulfilling the latter.

- The various elements of the marketing mix (i.e. product, place, promotion and price) must individually and collectively support the objectives of the business.

- Branding is everything you do consistently with the product; it is not just the logo.

- Distinctive and imaginative packaging is one of the simplest ways to differentiate your product effectively.

- Products should be rebranded when they fall under the banner of a quality product that is not being accepted by the target market.

- The realm of value-added services is one area that small businesses can be bigger in.

- Promotion is the tool for communicating with customers and informing them about how their needs will be met.

- For public relations to work well, the story you are pushing must be newsworthy.

- Sales promotion works in short, sharp bursts.

SUMMARY *continued*

- Set your pricing objectives to do one of three things: maximize sales, maximize profit or maintain the status quo.

- Set up a distribution channel that will allow your product to move as efficiently as possible up the line to the targeted customer.

5.3 IMPLEMENTING YOUR MARKETING BLUEPRINT

Now that you have written down the proposed strategies for the four elements of the marketing mix (i.e. product, price, promotion and place), you are now in a position to combine these strategies with time-related details and projected costs. This will then transform the broad strategic plan into a pragmatic action plan which, when implemented, can be done so at an acceptable level of risk.

The action plan will only be complete with the inclusion of the following details:

1. Timing details – outlining when each step is to be implemented.

2. Costing details – costing each stage of the action plan.

3. Personnel details – specifying the responsibilities of each staff member.

4. Specific details – charting exact tactical details for each stage of the action plan.

In short, you need answers to: who does what, when, where, how and at what cost.

Figure 5.5 on the next page is a template for an Action Plan Grid for your convenience.

To facilitate a seamless approach when implementing your action plan, a flowchart can be designed showing the logical and chronological sequence for each key task.

The flowchart can be used to itemize each task, the time that is required, as well as the costs associated with each task. A flowchart will enable you to foresee potential trouble spots and the consequences of certain tasks not performed properly.

5.4 JUSTIFIABLE RISK

Once an action plan is designed, the business must examine the level of risk to see if the plan is justifiable. Some key markers for evaluation of risk level include:

- Return on Investment

- Payback Period for Initial Investment

- Level of Gearing Ratio

(Action Plan Template)	Key Tasks to be Performed	Key Timelines - Start/Close	Who Per- forms the Task	Key Outcomes of Task	Costs and Resources Used	Other Key Information
January						
February						
March						
April						
May						
June						
July						
August						
September						
October						
November						
December						

Fig 5.5: Action Plan Grid

KEEP IN MIND

If the risk is justifiable, implement the action plan.

If not, abort or redesign the action plan.

It has been said that business and risk go hand in hand. Although a certain level of risk is considered justifiable, with regard to projected earnings, excessively high levels of risk are not acceptable and plans that expose the business to such risk levels should not be pursued.

Return on Investment

Return on Investment (R.O.I.) is the ratio of net profit to total investment. For example, if a business makes a net profit of $60,000 in a given year and the total investment required for setting up the business (leasing, stocks, overheads etc.) was $300,000, then the R.O.I.= 60,000/300,000 = 20%. Usually anything under 20% is unacceptable, as it means it will take longer than 5 years to recoup your initial investment.

Successful business leaders have perennially stressed the importance of R.O.I. as a critical component of business performance ahead of both income and profit.

There are many companies who have gone broke, despite making seemingly high levels of income, because the cost of running the business was too high.

Payback Period for Initial Investment

If the money invested in the business is $300,000 and the net profit = $60,000/year then the payback period is

5 years. Generally 5 years or less is considered an acceptable pay back time.

Level of Gearing Ratio

This ratio measures the ratio of borrowed funds to total investment.

If a business borrows $10,000 to start up and contributes $30,000 of its own, the ratio would be 10,000/40,000 = 25%.

Clearly, the higher the ratio, the greater is the burden due to the principle and interest repayments. This risk is further augmented in times of high interest rates. Generally speaking, more than 50% leverage is considered a high-risk venture.

SUMMARY

- Once the strategy for the four elements of the marketing mix (i.e. the 4 Ps) is completed, a comprehensive action plan containing tactical elements should be formulated.

- No business is devoid of risk, although differentiation between justifiable and unjustifiable risk should be understood.

- Key markers of risk evaluation such as Return on Investment should be routinely performed.

CHAPTER 6

STAGE D:
FEEDBACK FUNCTION
FOR YOUR MARKETING
BLUEPRINT

It was meant to be a ping pong table, but who cares, it looks good enough to sit on.

The **control or feedback function** is an essential feedback process the business uses to closely monitor and evaluate actual performance as compared to planned performance. The purpose for using the Control Function is twofold:

1. The business can monitor all marketing activities to ensure they are working to plan.

2. If any aspect is not working to plan, the business will be in a good position to respond quickly and effectively by making any appropriate adjustments.

The control function looks at all areas of performance including sales figures (in units or dollars), cost for all areas of the business and levels of profitability. It gives precise marketing and financial information, some of which cannot be obtained from a balance sheet or Profit & Loss statement.

6.1   KEY COMPARISON METRICS

The actual format or structure of analysis used will vary from business to business. Although there is no definitive format, the general principle here is that you should examine all the key parameters which you believe will reasonably give you greater understanding of what is happening in your business and why.

Examples of comparison metrics include:

- Actual and projected dollar sales data, broken down by department, by product line, by day-week-month, by season, by salesman, by sales team, etc.

- Actual and projected sales (units), broken down by similar criteria as above.

- Actual and projected costs, broken down by similar criteria as above.

- Actual and projected profit figures, broken down by similar criteria as above.

- Actual and projected sales per product and/or per product line, broken down by similar criteria as above.

On the next page is a table for charting actual and projected figures for each key area, as well as variances. These variances will need to be scrutinized so that appropriate changes can be identified and subsequently implemented.

Specific Item Being Reviewed	Planned Perfor- mance	Actual Perfor- mance	Variance	Postulated Reasons for the Variance	Changes to be Imple- mented

Figure 6.1: Variance Analysis Table

There can often be justifiable reasons why the original numbers projected do not come close to the actual numbers achieved. For example, industrial action beyond your control may affect the supply of key components, cause supplier problems and a fall in consumer demand.

When variations from planned performance occur, it must be quickly picked up and specifically identified with a view to correcting the situation. If, for example, the error occurred because one of the key assumptions (see section 4.4) was incorrect, then it must be adjusted accordingly to reflect a more appropriate approach.

No matter how precise a marketing blueprint and its subsequent implementation, given the changing nature of the business environment, ongoing and accurate feedback is needed to monitor and evaluate performance with the aim of maintaining control over all areas of the business.

Figure 6.2 is a typical budget and variance analysis chart for a business, which in this case, is from the Genesic Company (2004).

	Jan	Feb	Mar	Apr	May	Jun	Jul	Aug	Sept	Oct	Nov	Dec	TOTAL
					Market Budget and Variance Analysis for Genesic Product Range 2004								(000's)
Diaries	12												12
Rep Bonus	12												12
Media Advertising		20	10	10	20	10	10	10	10				100
Media Work up		10			10								20
Branding Promotional items	75	20						40					135
Direct Mail	13	12			25					25			75
Agency Fees	8	3	1	1	1	2	3	2	1	1	1	1	23
A4 Brochures		10						10					20
A5 Brochures		10						10					20
Campaign Work up Fee			30										30
Written Materials	25	0						25					50
Other printed		5						10					15
Workshop - design					42								42
Workshop - running					23	23	23	23	23	23			138
Conference - Materials								10					10
Training manuals		5						5					10
Focus Groups		35											35
Key Opinion Leader Forum			25	50		25	25	25					150
Cost of accommodation for meeting				25									25
Congresses						20		20					40
E Business			30								5		35
Competitors													0
Market Research		5											5
Publicity													0
Other initiatives					20					10			30
Allied Sponsorships		10											10
Storage/Freight of Materials	4	4	4	4	4	4	4	4	4	4	4	3	47
Customer Feedback forum				4	4	4	4	4					20
other miscellaneous costs	13	2											15
													0
													0
													0
	160	146	105	114	139	78	179	88	73	33	5	4	1124
													1124
Overall Total					1300								
Sales Force Discretionary spend					176								
Balance for Marketing Activities					1124								
				Deficit / surplus	0								

Figure 6.2: Example of a Typical Budget and
Variance Analysis Chart for a Business

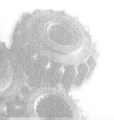

6.2 OTHER KEY METRICS

Many of the key financial **metrics** (or measures of performance), have already been mentioned in this chapter. However, some non-financial markers are also critical in conducting a thorough evaluation. These markers can include attitudinal, behavioral and evolutionary aspects that are measurable and important to the future of the business.

Examples include:

- Perceptions of customers: How do customers see the business and its products today versus a year ago? Has the perception changed and, if so, how?

- Customer retention rates: How successful is the business in retaining its key customers? Is the number of customers who are loyal by design increasing or decreasing?

- Evolutionary Index: How has the business grown in the last year compared to the overall market within which it operates?

- Growth Index: How have different products, product ranges or departments within the business grown compared to the overall business in the last year?

- Ratio of inquiries to converted sales: Has the ratio of converting customer calls (of whatever type) to sales increased or decreased in the last year?

- Customer trust index: Specifically in relation to trust, has your ongoing customer research found increasing or decreasing levels of customer trust over the last year?

- Customer satisfaction: How satisfied are the customers based on all their dealings with the business in the last year?

- Intention to increase purchasing levels: This is a key measure of what proportion of your customers have signaled an intention to increase their use of your products in the future. This is a critical indicator, as it is well recognized that it is generally easier to get an existing customer to use more product than to get a non-user to start using it.

- Reach and frequency analysis: This indicates how effective the promotional activities have been and how often and how well the key promotional messages have reached the target audience.

- Retention of message: How well has the target market understood and retained the key promotional messages?

By using research-based feedback (as discussed in Chapter 3), you will be able to gain an even greater understanding of the true performance of your business.

6.3   NOW FOR THE FUNKIER CROWD...

When presenting sales data to your employees and/or suppliers, you could use financial tables, graphs or a combination of approaches. There is no right or wrong approach.

A sales analysis can potentially be dry to present. When a snapshot is required, you may want to consider using 'dashboards.' These dashboards are very simple templates, which allow you to present key markers of success in a fun way. Below is a hypothetical example of a dashboard for a fictitious telecommunications company, Phonetronics, which sells mobile phones.

The use of these types of dashboards are effective in that they can effectively gain people's attention and are able to convey key performance data in a non threatening way, to people who are often not financially minded.

The templates themselves are freely available on the Internet at: http://office.microsoft.com/clipart

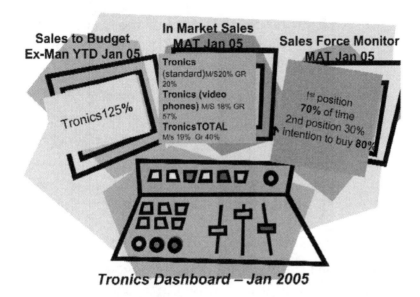

Tronics Dashboard – Jan 2005

Figure 6.3: Product Performance Dashboard

Yeah. Right, sure there's growth in learning

KEEP IN MIND

The only true strategic failure occurs when nothing is learned from prior experience. Anything learned is a step closer to achieving eventual success.

SUMMARY

Following the implementation of the action plan, the business establishes a control function to review planned versus actual performance.

From the variances uncovered (whether positive or negative), the business is able to consider the reasons for any variance and what adjustments need to be made.

10 THINGS YOU SHOULD NEVER DO

- Assume you know what your customers' needs are
- Underestimate the short comings of your business
- Try to market your product to everyone
- Take your customers for granted
- Hire slick salespeople with poor listening skills
- Design your marketing plan in a vacuum
- Leave weaker areas of the business alone
- Launch into expensive research every time
- Dwell on poor performance
- Stress out completely and lose your work/life balance

GLOSSARY OF TERMS

ADVERTISING: Paid form of non-personal presentation of product.

ADVERTISING ALLOWANCE: Reduced product price to members of the distribution channel as an incentive to further promote a product.

ADVERTISING OBJECTIVES: Predetermination of what the business wishes to achieve through advertising.

BRANDING: Identification of a product by the use of any recognizable word, letter, symbol or other designation.

COMPARATIVE ADVERTISING: Designed to highlight specific advantages one brand has over another in a given product class.

COMPETITIVE ADVERTISING: Designed to drive demand for specific brands.

COMPREHENSIVE ANALYSIS: First stage of the marketing planning process, which answers the question about what position a business is currently in. It examines both the internal workings of the business, as well as, the external market it operates in.

CONSUMERISM: A movement towards customers gaining increasing levels of awareness and general product knowledge. The advent of the Internet has fueled this movement to far greater heights.

CONTROL FUNCTION: A feedback process by which the business is able to compare actual and planned performance with a view to uncover any variances that may occur in any area of the business operations.

CONVENIENCE GOODS: Required, simple product lines the consumer wants to obtain with minimal effort.

COPY: The contents of an advertisement.

CULTURE: The sum of all the enthusiasm, imagination, and dynamic energy of all the people who are at the business.

CURRENCY EXCHANGE RATE: The rate that one monetary currency will be exchanged for another at any given point in time. For example 1 Australian dollar = 0.75 US dollars.

DISCRETIONARY INCOME: Level of income that is available to a consumer to spend on purchasing goods and services, after taking into account mandatory expenses such as income tax and cost of living expenses.

ECONOMIC GROWTH RATE: The rate at which a nation has increased its ability to produce goods and services. It is usually expressed as an annual percentage over the previous year's rate.

ELASTIC DEMAND: Price responsive market where changes in price will cause an increase or decrease in product demand due to the homogeneous nature of the products.

EXTERNAL (MARKET) ANALYSIS: Analysis of the characteristics, size, and overall trends which currently prevail in the market that the business operates in.

FEEDBACK FUNCTION: Fourth and final module of the marketing planning process which looks critically at how well the marketing plan has been implemented and uncovers any variances between planned and actual performance. As well, it looks at possible explanations for these variances with the view of being better able to predict future performance.

FIXED COSTS: Costs that are fixed at the production or sales level.

HETEROGENEOUS PRODUCT: A product offering that is perceived by the customer as being different from other rival products or brands.

HOMOGENEOUS PRODUCT: A product offering that is perceived by the customer as being virtually the same as other rival options carrying with it no real advantage.

INELASTIC DEMAND: Price unresponsive markets, where increases in price cause little change in demand.

INFLATION (RATE): The rate of increase seen in the price of goods and services over a specific time frame (usually one year).

INSTITUTIONAL ADVERTISING: Designed to influence and shape people's perceptions and attitudes about an organization.

INTEREST RATES: The cost of borrowing money, usually expressed as an annual rate of the principle borrowed e.g. 7.00% per annum.

INTERNAL (BUSINESS) ANALYSIS: Analysis of the business examining its strengths and weaknesses as they relate to the market within which it operates.

KEY SUCCESS FACTORS: Those factors that are essential for a business to successfully meet the unmet needs of a given market segment.

LAGGARD: Late adopter of a given product relative to the initial customers who try the product when new to the market place.

MARKET ANALYSIS: The analysis of the market or external environment a business operates in, with a view to determining the uncontrollable opportunities and threats the business will face.

MARKETING: Systematic process by which the business identifies and meets the needs of its targeted customers.

MARKET INFORMATION: Essentially, information from market research, used for both strategic and tactical planning.

MARKETING MIX: A set of four controllable factors (i.e. product, price, promotion and place).

MARKETING BLUEPRINT: A formally written report that translates the desired marketing strategy into a systematic action plan with timelines, cost estimates and levels of risk required to implement the proposed strategy. This is traditionally the third module of the marketing planning process.

MARKETING PLANNING PROCESS: Systematic process that includes identifying the objectives of the business, the specific marketing plan to achieve the objectives and the control function to monitor how effectively the process has been applied.

MARKET PRICING POLICY: Policy whereby the business adopts the same product price relative to rival brands. Under these conditions the business competes on a non-pricing basis where product differences or other additional services differentiate the product, not the price.

MARKET RESEARCH: The process by which a business gathers and analyzes valuable market information as a basis for ongoing decision-making.

MARKET SEGMENT: Portion of the overall market that has been identified based on a specific unmet need shared by a subset of the population.

MARKET SEGMENTATON: The process of breaking up the entire market into a number of small sub-markets with similar needs based on a given set criteria. From these smaller sub-markets, a business can then select the most viable segments and develop marketing plans directed specifically at them.

MASS MARKETING: "Shot gun" approach to marketing where a business indiscriminately targets anyone within a given market, rather than specific groups of individuals with similar needs.

MATCHING PROCESS: Process of matching business resources with customer needs within market segments. From this the business is able to systematically identify those customer groups they are more likely to successfully deal with.

MONOPOLY: Situation where a business has almost total control of a given market or sub-market, at any given time because of a unique product.

OBJECTIVES MODULE: Second stage of the marketing planning process that examines the objectives the business sets itself to achieve.

OLIGOPOLY: Market where relatively small number of sellers control a market with similar product offerings.

OPPORTUNITY COST: The cost of not implementing the next best alternative.

PARETO'S LAW: States that 80% of all sales come from 20% of customers.

PENETRATION PRICING POLICY: Policy whereby the business adopts a lower product price relative to rival brands with the aim of increasing their market share.

PIONEERING ADVERTISING: Designed to build awareness and demand for new products or services.

PRIMARY DEMAND: Demand generated for a product class, but not a specific brand within that class.

PRIMARY INFORMATION: Data from market research which is specifically obtained to help in the decision making process, usually after all secondary sources of market information are exhausted.

PRODUCT ADVERTISING: Aims to sell a particular product offering.

PRODUCT LIFE CYCLE: The phases a product will pass through, from its introduction into the market as a new product to its decline at the end of its product life.

PRODUCT MANAGEMENT: The ongoing process of handling the changing needs of a product as it goes through the various stages of the product life cycle.

PROFIT ORIENTED PRICING STRATEGY: Business maximizes profits at the expense of market share by setting as high a price as the market will bear.

PROMOTION: Is the process by which the business can communicate with its customers and inform them on how their needs will be met.

PROMOTIONAL OBJECTIVES: Define what a business hopes to achieve through its promotional activities.

PUBLIC RELATIONS (or PUBLICITY): Unlike advertising is a form of promotion where the business has little control over what is said.

PURE COMPETITION: Competition situation where no business can directly influence the market as the products are seen to be homogeneous and, therefore, price responsive.

QUALITATIVE RESEARCH TECHNIQUE: In-depth individual responses based on high-gain, open-ended probing to gain insight from customer on beliefs, attitudes or behaviors.

QUANTITATIVE RESEARCH TECHNIQUE: Structured feedback using a more closed approach to validate the scope of the responses from qualitative research.

REMINDER ADVERTISING: Designed to remind customers of either an established brand or corporation.

RETURN ON INVESTMENT: Key financial measure of performance measured by dividing net profit over total investment to determine how many years it will take to fully pay the cost of the investment.

SALES PROMOTION: Special promotions the business offers, outside of its price, to customers and other members of the distribution chain.

SECONDARY INFORMATION: Information that already exists and is available to the business for use in putting together its marketing plan.

SEMI-VARIABLE COST: Cost that has both a fixed and variable component.

SHOPPING GOODS: Unlike convenience goods, these are more expensive goods that the customer is willing to invest effort in purchasing.

SKIMMING PRICING POLICY: Policy whereby a business adopts higher pricing levels to maximize profit because it holds some level of differentiation from rival products.

SMALL BUSINESS: The size of a business operation traditionally seen to having an annual dollar turnover of less than two million dollars.

SMASHING (or SMASHED) BRANDS: Occur when you are able to remove company or brand logos, and yet can still recognize that brand.

SPECIALTY GOODS: Products or services that the consumer has a high level of demand for and will spend significant resources to obtain.

STOCKING ALLOWANCES: Reduced product prices offered to retailers to stock new or existing products.

S.W.O.T. ANALYSIS: Analysis that examines both the internal strengths and weaknesses of the business as well as the external market derived opportunities and threats. The internal elements are deemed controllable, whereas the external elements are uncontrollable.

TARGET MARKET: A group of customers with the same or similar needs, which the business wishes to attract.

TOTAL COST: Sum of all variable, semi-variable and fixed costs.

UNEMPLOYMENT RATE: The percentage of the labor force who are unemployed at a given point and who are actively looking for work.

UNIQUE PRODUCT OFFERING: A distinguishing feature, benefit or aspect that sets a business product or service apart from the rest of the competition in that market.

UNMET CUSTOMER NEED: Recognized need of targeted customer that is either in part or wholly, as yet, unmet.

UNSOUGHT GOODS: Products that customers may have no awareness of and/or desire to purchase, at least in the first instance.

VALUE: A measure of how much worth the customer places on purchasing your product offering given the price they paid. The stronger the sense of product value, the stronger the sense of customer satisfaction is likely to be.

VARIABLE COST: Cost that varies directly with different levels of production or sales.

VOLUME ALLOWANCES: Reduced prices or rebates to members of the distribution channel based on the number of units purchased, as a means of motivating them to buy more stock.

ABOUT THE AUTHORS

CHRIS LEE BIOGRAPHY

Chris was born in and lived in South Korea. He later went on to study in the USA and did his Bachelors degree at The University of Arizona. Following this, Chris went on to obtain his Executive M.B.A in International Management from the internationally renowned Thunderbird - The Garvin School of International Management, Arizona. U.S.A.

He has subsequently worked and excelled in the business world for the last 17 years with leading multinational pharmaceutical companies such as Merck Sharpe and Dohme and Bristol-Myers Squibb.

He has reached the top of the proverbial business tree with postings as Managing Director, in both various countries including China, Korea and Australia. Incredibly he has built a track record that reflects record levels of achievement and company performance despite operating in depressed economies where other comparable companies were concurrently recording record losses and turnover in the same period.

Away from business, Chris has led an extraordinary life. He has achieved the rating of a fifth dan black belt in Taekwondo, being one of only a very few individuals globally to achieve this lofty status. (Legendary martial artist Bruce Lee was a third dan).

He also represented the United States in Taekwondo at the 1988 Olympics in Seoul.

Moreover, he is a recognised and published master chef, who interestingly boasts a personal collection of 3,000 cook books. A true world traveler, Chris has visited every country bar one, North Korea.

Chris Lee's first book titled *Emotional Management in Business* has been a tremendous success and became an instant #1 best seller, outselling even Jack Welsh at the time during its release in 2004. The book broke new ground in terms of outlining how to motivate people to perform to new heights. And with it the term "Romantic Management" was born.

His unique approach and skills have made him instantly recognised in Asia and he was voted the most successful manager in his industry in Korea where he took his company with less than US$3 M in sales to more than US$100 M in less than 5 years despite a national recession, recording performances of up to 700% of budget expectation.

Locally renowned Korean entrepreneur and celebrity Sohn Ji Chang was quoted as saying, "In the US they have Jack Welsh but here we have Chris Lee."

Chris Lee is regarded as the top managerial mind in Korea and one of the greatest strategic thinkers globally.

He is now the Managing Director of global giant Bayer Healthcare in China which has quickly become the battle ground, where most companies in the Fortune 500 are battling for a toe hold in the world's fastest growing market.

Under his dynamic leadership, Bayer Healthcare has now become the fastest growing multinational health care company in China with an extraordinary growth rate of 32%.

This feat made even more extraordinary by the fact that the result was not helped with the launch of any new products during this period to drive sales.

This after spending the previous two years as Managing Director of cardiovascular powerhouse Bristol- Myers Squibb Pharmaceuticals in Melbourne, Australia.

His success in business is revolutionary, being the youngest Sales and Marketing Director (at 27) and the youngest Managing Director (at 31) in his country's history.

Chris, now 41, lives with his wife Elaine and son, Eugene, in China and has now completed his much awaited new book, *Marketing Works: Unlocking Big Company Strategies for Small Business.*

DANIELE LIMA BIOGRAPHY

Daniele Lima was born and educated in Melbourne, Australia. He has studied extensively in all areas of business and is a Business graduate from Swinburne Institute of Technology, Melbourne, majoring in marketing and economics.

In a twenty year career, he has worked in virtually all areas of business in large and small companies alike, including Caltex Petroleum, Metrail and Bristol-Myers Squibb.

He has held numerous managerial postings and has had wide ranging experiences including positions such as National Sales Manager, Regional Training Manager and Senior Product Marketing Manager. He has won multiple industry awards and years later, still holds sales and marketing related records. As well, Daniele has developed and runs the renowned Road Scholars Sales & Marketing training programs.

He currently is the head of Gotham Enterprises Sales and Marketing, a consulting firm in Melbourne, Australia and is heavily involved in all aspects of sales, marketing and training.

He has been an Associate of the Australian Institute of Marketing for fifteen years and is a Certified Practicing Marketer (C.P.M).

Daniele, now 43, continues to live and work in his beloved hometown of Melbourne.

CONTACT THE AUTHORS

Any enquiries for marketing
consultations with the authors
can be made via:

www.roadscholarstraining.com

BONUS WORKBOOK

FREE BONUS

Marketing Works Workbook

Make your marketing work by implementation TODAY.
Grab your FREE Marketing Works Workbook at
www.Morgan-James.com/workbook

9 781600 370090